How to Start Your Dog Boarding Business

What to know about dogs, kennels, and the business

Sarah Clark

Second Edition

While all attempts have been made to verify the information provided in this publication, neither the author nor the publisher assume any responsibility for errors, omissions, or contrary interpretations of the subject matter herein. The views expressed are those of the author alone and should not be taken as expert instruction or commands.

Everything in this book is based on the author's experience. Nothing should be taken as a substitute for your own judgment.

ISBN – 978-1-948158-12-1 epub
ISBN – 978-1-948158-13-8 paperback

To Simone, for bringing two people together

Table of Contents

INTRODUCTION

This book is about how I started a successful, home-based, dog boarding business in the middle of nowhere. The book is also about whether you, wherever you are, should do the same.

You can look on the internet and get all the information you need about how to make a physical kennel. But the why behind it, the how behind it, the practicality behind the physical kennel, that's really what I am going to talk about.

Once I was in your position and knew little about boarding dogs. So in this revised and expanded second edition, I have added new sections and more resources to help you.

The first new section is about how to understand the dog community where you live. The second is about marketing, because it doesn't matter how good you are, if you have no clients. The third new section is about starting and managing your business.

Because I love animals, I want there to be good places where people can board their dogs. And because I am out of the business now, I have no secrets to hold back. But if you talk to people who are in the business, they are not as likely to share the lessons they learned through hard knocks. They have no reason to help the competition.

Before you spend a dime on your dog boarding business, I want to give you the thought process you need to consider. If you buy this book, I want to save you money, effort, and time because you can learn from my experience. Think of my experience as your own secret weapon.

I want you to succeed. Or fail. Because if this book helps you understand why this is not a business for you, I will have succeeded just as much as if you find the book encouraging. The problems I solved will not be exactly the same as the problems you need to solve, though many of them will be.

This book has four parts: design, implementation, day-to-day operations, and entering the business. In case you are wondering, I also boarded cats and I will discuss cat boarding, too.

In the design section, I will tell you how I designed and built my kennel and offer suggestions about how you can, too. In the other three sections, I will cover topics ranging from setting up your business to acquiring customers to handling daily operations. Along the way, I will tell some personal stories because lessons from stories are easiest to remember.

The table of contents is only the briefest indication of all the topics I will cover.

Let me assure you; I didn't come to this field as some kind of dog whisperer. In fact, I didn't grow up with dogs. I owned my first dog, a golden retriever, just three years before I started my pet boarding business.

Here's my story.

I was moved to a new state, pretty much against my will. I didn't think it was a good idea to go to a place I knew nothing about, where I wouldn't have a job and neither would my husband. We moved to be close to his parents who had relocated after they retired.

My husband and I bought a house on the outskirts of a town which was the county seat. Though it was a county seat, the town had a population of just 2,000 and the entire county had only 22,000 people.

After we settled in, my husband got a job which required travel, and I went downtown to look for work. The first place I applied was the local newspaper.

The editor hired me to do ad layouts. That had been his wife's job, but he wanted to give her a break and get things done faster. At least that's what he told me.

The editor usually held forth from his office with the office door open. When he wanted something, he just shouted. Normally, his wife was right outside the door, but on this occasion, I was closer than his wife.

He hollered, "What's another word for a nickname or what you call somebody?"

"Nom de plume," I shot back.

"Doesn't fit," he said.

"Moniker," I said. There was a pause.

"Nobody likes a smartass," he said.

Things were worse with his wife. If I laid out an ad, she wanted the text moved 1.5 mm to the right. On the next layout, she wanted the ad moved 1.5 mm to the left. If I used an Arial font, she wanted Helvetica. If I used Helvetica, she wanted Arial. Nothing I did was ever right for her.

After a few weeks, I gave up.

It didn't help that I didn't have a rural drawl like my employers. I speak with the national accent of radio and

TV people, which means I don't sound like I come from any particular place. But this experience made me feel like even more of an outsider.

I only had two job ideas left. First, I thought about doing something computer related since I had experience installing computer systems. The second idea was an ill-formed notion about working with dogs. I decided to walk down to city hall, talk to people in the offices, and ask which business they thought might work in the area.

They all voted for computers.

But they also told me a man had just opened a computer business in town. He could do everything I could do, and repair computers as well. I didn't think I could compete head-to-head with someone who had a storefront location and that kind of expertise. I also didn't know if there would be enough business in town for both of us.

When I asked the people in the courthouse if they thought there was a market for a dog boarding business, no one thought so. But it was my final idea, and I plunged ahead.

Did my idea work?

Let me put it this way: boarding dogs, I earned an income three times greater than that of a full-time employee at the local newspaper. The nearest town of size was a city of 150,000 a hundred miles away. Yet many people drove that hundred miles, bypassing other kennels along the way, to board with me.

My dog's veterinarian boarded dogs, yet when he and his family went out of town, they boarded their two dogs with me. I ran my business, called The Pet Hotel, for five years and left only when my husband got a job offer in a larger city.

People who care about pets care about where they leave their pets. With most service businesses, the reason the business is successful is linked to the specific person running the business. You are the key. To put it another way, do you go to the hair salon for the salon, or for the stylist?

Part of this job is reassuring people their pet will be safe. If you are cut out for this, you will be telling the truth because their pet will be safe and well-cared-for with you. You don't necessarily need to be a people person. You just need to inspire confidence in pet owners.

What I'm saying is, you can fake it with people, if you're not a great people person, but you can't fake it with the dogs. You have to like dogs. You are dealing with an entity that is alive, has great emotional value to people, and can be unpredictable.

If you haven't done this before, you might dive right into the "how to build it" without thinking, "Is this the right choice for me?" Remember, your clients are choosing you. You have to be a confident, likable person to your clients.

As with anything, unless you know the details, the business may look good on the surface, but the devil is always in the details. Until you look at the details, you won't know if boarding dogs is for you. There's a downside to being a supermodel, and a downside to being a celebrity. There are downsides to the job you have right now. And you know the downside because you know the details.

If you aren't the kind of person who cleans up after your dog when you walk it, this isn't the job for you. If you like to sleep in on the weekends, this is not the job for you. If you want to work an eight-hour day, five days a week, this is not the job for you. But if you love dogs, it may be.

What you are trying to build up is a number of good clients with good dogs that you can take care of for years and years. You want dogs in the sizes and breeds you are comfortable with, from good pet owners. The sweet spot in this business is indoor, housebroken, house pets. These are the dogs that are used to being handled.

My final thought is this: start small. Once you decide this is the field for you, I suggest starting on a reasonable scale. Many small businesses fail because they initially start as if they are already making $100k a year.

Construction people are more than willing to let you start too big as long as their money is guaranteed. But you don't want to start out with a $100,000 loan or a second mortgage on your house and no customers. But you can start with a one car garage, a walkout basement, a small outbuilding. If you have one of those, you have the basis to begin.

If you don't have those, you can start with pet sitting or dog walking. Get bonded. Get cash coming in where the only outlay is time and gas. Or sign up with Rover or Wag! and begin pet sitting in your home. However you start, the safest way to begin is on a small scale.

That's it for the introduction. Let's begin and get into the nitty-gritty of how I started and built my business.

PART ONE

DESIGN

Though what I did seems natural now, at the time, it took a lot of thought.

What did I start with? No experience in the dog boarding business, no experience growing up with dogs, and three years' experience with a single dog.

What I had was five acres of land, with two rather ramshackle outbuildings behind my house. One building had good bones, and the other could be rehabilitated with a lot of work. *Perhaps,* I thought, *one could be torn down and made into an addition to the other.*

The problem was, the buildings were about 50 yards from the house, and there was no path to them, no source of water, and no electricity. Consequently, heating, air conditioning, and lighting would be a problem.

On the east side of the house was a gravel road leading to several small farms and homes. In front of the house was a two-lane blacktop with a pasture across the road. On the west side, the property extended for about two and a half acres, but it was a downhill slope, and for that reason, unusable.

At least, with no near neighbors, barking dogs would not be a problem.

I knew I would need to go outside to take care of dogs regardless of the weather. That would mean working sometimes in snow or rain. Security of the dogs would be paramount. How could I make sure the dogs were always safe from animals like coyotes, raccoons, and snakes? Coyotes can be dangerous, especially when food is scarce, and raccoons can eviscerate a dog or scratch its eyes out.

The greatest snake danger in the area was from copperheads, which are poisonous, and from nonpoisonous black snakes, which are powerful constrictors. Owls and hawks might be a problem for the littlest dogs. They might require a special pen with netting above if I left them alone for a while. And, of course, any concentration of bees or hornets could pose a risk to dogs.

I did have some assets. After my husband and I moved in, we generously fenced in the backyard with a four-foot-high chain-link fence. I wanted a safe area for my dog, Einstein, and I thought maybe I would get a second dog. At the time, I had no idea I would be building a dog boarding business.

We also had a car-and-a-half garage attached to the house by a breezeway. When we moved in, the garage was unusable. The gravel road behind the garage was at a higher elevation, and over time, dirt and mud had accumulated on the garage floor.

Apparently, the previous owners often left the garage door open and parked their cars alongside the garage or on the crescent shaped driveway in front of the house.

When I cleaned out the garage, I was pleased to find a concrete floor. Perhaps that could be the basis of my kennel.

Two Basic Kennel Models

There are two basic models for a kennel. One is the classic indoor/outdoor combination where a building is divided into pens, with each pen having a doggy door leading to a fenced outside run. In this arrangement, dogs are confined in separate pens, with each dog having its own run. The dogs can hear and usually see each other in the runs, but they are kept apart.

In an indoor/outdoor kennel, the floor of the building is concrete, and the run is usually either concrete or pea gravel. The advantage of concrete is ease of cleaning, but it comes with two disadvantages. The first is expense. The second disadvantage is that dogs used to being on carpet, linoleum, and grass can't be left for long periods on such a harsh surface.

In addition, many dogs won't pee or poop on a hard surface like concrete. It depends on what the dog is used to. So while you think a run will eliminate messes in the kennel, it may not. Some dogs may not know how to use a doggy door. In cold climates in winter, you won't be able to hose down concrete. In summer, you have to be aware how hot the surface may get, as it can burn sensitive paws.

Pea gravel has even more disadvantages. Though you can wash urine away, as with concrete, it is much more difficult to collect stool. You will constantly throw gravel away with feces, especially when a dog has diarrhea. In addition, pea gravel is a digger's paradise, and when a house pet is boarded at a kennel with a pea gravel run, the dog is likely to go home with red, swollen, and cut paws.

Dogs often won't stop themselves from doing hurtful things, especially when running and playing with other dogs on an unfamiliar surface.

The other boarding possibility was an indoor kennel with a pen for each dog and an outside exercise area. This model allows for dogs to mingle and be exercised together, if you choose, though each dog will have to be led into the exercise area from the kennel.

That is the model I decided to follow, for several reasons:

First, it was less expensive than building an indoor/outdoor kennel. I wanted a kennel scaled to my business volume, and as yet the concept was unproven.

I also knew I could build pens in the garage and use the backyard fence we already had. It was fortunate that we had fenced such a generous area behind the house. The downside was the fence was only four feet high. I had some concerns that a dog might attempt to go over the fence. So I came up with a workaround.

If I thought a dog might try to jump the fence, I could attach a cable to its collar and leave the other end free. This would allow the dog plenty of freedom, yet the friction from dragging a cable would keep a dog from leaping out of confinement. Dog tie-out cables are sold in standard lengths like 10, 15, and 20 feet, and I would select a length based on the size of the dog.

In the five years I ran my dog boarding business, not one dog jumped over the fence and only rarely did a dog need a cable. The caveat with cables is this: If you attach a cable to a dog's collar, you need to make sure to watch over the dog. Many dogs have no experience being at the end of a cable and could get themselves tangled up.

Another thing I liked about the short fence height was that it didn't interfere with the view. It seemed reasonable for the property. As fence height increases, the area where dogs are confined begins to look foreboding. It looks less and less like a place where a person with a housebroken, house pet would want to leave their dog and more like a prison.

Also, I knew an excessively tall fence could be seen as a negative by a potential buyer if we ever moved.

There were two more advantages to the kind of kennel I would have. By using an existing building, if my plans didn't work out, I could convert the kennel back into a much-improved garage. If you are going to construct an outbuilding or buy a two-car garage to use as a kennel, you will still have a perfectly serviceable building after its kennel days are over.

Equally as important, and this is something you can point out to pet parents when they view your facility, with this arrangement, each dog would get personalized handling many times a day. Though this arrangement is more labor intensive for you, it's a much more desirable arrangement for the pet and pet owner.

Dogs getting a reasonable amount of exercise will behave better in their pens. They will thrive on being able to run around and play on grass, as well as through your contact and attention.

I still had two problems to figure out: how to configure the garage as a kennel, and from the standpoint of workflow, how to figure out if my layout would work?

Space in the garage was limited. There was room for shelving inside the door to the garage, but if I had a desk, it would reduce the number of pens I could build. For that reason, I decided to forego a desk.

When a pet and pet parent arrived, I would meet them with a clipboard in hand. The clipboard would contain my boarding agreement and a pet information sheet, where I gathered additional information about the pet and owner. More about these two in the next chapter.

The shelving in the garage I would use for the food and treats the dog came with, as well as for odds and ends. The dog's leash and any toys the dog's owners brought would go in a small plastic basket on top of the pen where each dog was boarded, though that is getting a little ahead of myself.

My records would be kept permanently in a home office in the house. It wasn't the ideal solution, but it had one positive unintended effect. Often a pet parent needed to come inside my house to complete a transaction. Having the records in my home reinforced the personalization of the business and made it seem as if the pet was being boarded by family.

The challenges of the garage were multiple. The door to the garage opened onto a breezeway which connected to the house. The house and garage were also joined by a short white fence with a gate.

The breezeway provided shelter as dogs arrived, but lots of work needed to be done to the interior of the garage. To make it attractive, with my husband's help, I installed paneling.

Between the garage wall and the paneling, we stuffed insulation. We covered the large garage door with insulation and paneled it over as well. Next, we added a ceiling of waferboard and painted the ceiling and walls white. I wanted the kennel to be light and bright. For durability, I painted the concrete floor with a gray sealant paint.

When a dog goes into a pen, the pen must be an immovable object. You might be surprised how much a determined dog can move, and it's essential that a dog does not have a belief there is a way out.

In the garage, I had enough room for two rows of pens with a 4-foot walkway in between. As you entered from the doorway, pens for small and medium-sized dogs were on the left, pens for medium and large-sized dogs were on the right. The small pens were 3 x 4 feet while the large pens were 4 x 6. There were 13 pens total.

My pens were home-built using 2 x 4s as framework. The walls between the pens were made of corrugated steel cut 4 feet high and overlapped to prevent exposed edges. The back wall was also covered with corrugated steel to prevent dogs from gnawing on the wood paneling. The top of each pen was covered with chain-link stretched over a wooden frame.

Doors to the pens were constructed on a wood frame covered with wire, with a diagonal crosspiece reinforcing the door for strength. Each door was hinged in two places and secured with a barrel bolt lock, top and bottom. There was no exposed area where a dog could injure a paw or mouth.

The pens were attached to each other as one solid unit, nailed to the back wall, and nailed to the concrete floor. They were strong and sturdy. If you leaned against them, there was no give.

I had a good reason for building 4-foot-high pens. Six-foot pens would cost more, 50 percent more. In addition, with 6-foot pens, there would be no vista, no sightline, and no perception of space. The kennel would look like a room full of closets.

Ventilation was yet another reason for 4-foot pens. The garage had had a light fixture in the center. I replaced that light with a lighted ceiling fan to circulate air. Importantly, the ceiling fan would provide uniform distribution of cool air in the summer and warm air in the winter to each pen.

The garage had a series of small windows above the pens. In a center window, I installed a small air conditioner. In front of the kennel, by the door, I installed a wall-mounted electric heater. When there were only a few dogs in the kennel during the winter, I put them in pens closest to the heater. When there were more dogs, I used the ceiling fan to distribute the warm air.

I placed a rug runner in front and down the length of the kennel so owners would not be standing on hard concrete. I put curtains on the garage windows and pictures on the wall. When I was done, the kennel had a homey quality to it. It felt cozy.

Designing your kennel is all a process of thought. You consider one idea, then think how that might impact something else. In the end, you end up with the best you can do with what you have.

Following that process, I realized I still had one unanswered workflow issue. A single exercise yard would be a problem while working with multiple dogs.

To solve this problem, I created four 10 x 10 foot chain-link fenced areas within the larger yard. They were in a row, with the nearest one abutting the outer wall of the garage. Actually, one of them was 10 x 14. This was because tree roots prevented placement of a corner post, and I didn't want to lose the shade the tree provided.

With four fenced in areas, each opening into the large exercise yard, I could work with five dogs separately or even more if some dogs could be grouped together. On the other hand, if there was a dog that didn't get along with other dogs, I could leave an empty pen between it and the others.

I put my kennel in the garage and hand-built everything because, with no business, that is what I could afford. When you are small, with only a limited investment, you can see the next step, the next extension of buildings or services. You know what your income is and what you can afford to do.

In addition, the traditional design of a kennel with individual runs seemed sterile to me. It lacks eye appeal. At most of the operations I've seen, I would not like to leave my beloved house dog.

Similarly, I would not want to board my dog at most vet facilities. He would be confined in a cage and see only a few people for a short period of time over nights and weekends. He might be exposed to a sick pet.

As you can tell, my plan was not perfect or state-of-the-art, but it worked. Your plan may not be perfect either. That doesn't mean it won't work.

The Easiest Way to Start

I think the easiest way to start a pet boarding business is as a home business, on a property you have or live on. Don't start way beyond what you have, but dream a little. How can you make it work with what you have?

Do you have a barn or unused section of a barn or other outbuilding? Do you have someone who can lay concrete or put a kit building together? What makes logical sense based on the lay of your land?

If you want an instant, ready-to-use kennel design, search the internet. If you can't shell out a lot of money, workarounds and elbow grease can solve many problems. To get expert advice, visit home supply stores, hardware stores, and lumberyards. Often they have people with years of construction experience.

Look for reclaimed barn wood and secondhand materials. Salvage yards often have lumber and hardware at a huge savings. Or start with a prefab building with a couple of windows. If it doesn't work out, you have gained added storage space.

Or get a two-car garage. Worst case scenario, you have increased the value of your property by a large garage. Use some foresight in what you plan. Try to make whatever you plan into something which adds value to your property.

And when your plan does work out and you get so busy you need a larger building, reconfigure the old kennel. Move the working kennel to its new building and let the old kennel revert to being a two-car garage or whatever it was.

The main idea is, build value into your property.

I deliberately haven't included detailed plans of my kennel because it was a one-off. It was my particular solution to a particular situation.

For your kennel, I suggest this: Take what you have, what you think you can spend, and use Pinterest, YouTube, and other internet sites to locate commercial and non-commercial kennel plans. See what's out there.

Start sketching possibilities. Don't be afraid to start small. Think of the basics—heat, AC, light. Where will people stand when they bring their dog? What will you need as you take the dog in?

If you live in an apartment in Manhattan, you may not be able to start a dog boarding kennel. But you could live in Manhattan and start dog walking or pet sitting in the building you are in. You could offer overnight or weekend pet boarding in your own apartment and during holidays like Thanksgiving, Black Friday, Christmas, and New Year's Eve.

If you have a home with a fenced yard, you can start by advertising "dog boarding in my home." You can begin with one dog at a time and advertise on Craigslist or Facebook. To see how other people do this, get a Gmail account and set an alert for "dog boarding." Every day your email will contain a trove of ideas.

In an urbanized area with limited space, you might consider starting a kennel that specializes in toy or small dogs. Owners of these pets may be more comfortable knowing there are no large dogs on the premises. If you are planning to buy a house in the country, think about how you could start your kennel when you buy that house in a couple of years.

Starting a kennel is a bit like opening a daycare. If you don't know if the idea is right for you, you can start with a little babysitting. You are in business in a micro way, and your modest start will inspire the next step.

Now that I've told you how I began, I still faced a big question: Would anyone come? Would anyone want to come? That's really a matter of implementation, which is the subject of the next chapter.

PART TWO

IMPLEMENTATION

The idea of starting a boarding kennel is moot unless you can figure out what you can do, where you are, with what you have. Many people will be in a rural or less developed area, or getting a piece of land to build their kennel. But that is not an absolute requirement. Can you board dogs in the location where you are? That's the first question.

In addition, the business has to be based on who you are. Can you physically do the job? Do you have a health problem? Allergies? Any limitations that can't be overcome?

Clients will be choosing you, so the business must be right for you. What will make you a more confident and attractive person to clients? What will make your facility attractive to them? Those are issues to think about.

Over time, I found, the strongest recommendations come from the dogs themselves.

I'm thinking now of two boarders, Bob and Max, a Dalmatian and a Labrador retriever who would pull their owner, a local attorney, from his car to my front gate begging to be let in.

I'm thinking of Toby, a 110 pound Akita, whose owner was a strapping young man with a muscular upper body, yet he struggled to control Toby's rush to my kennel.

Then there were Boo-Boo, the Pomeranian, and Nietzsche, an Alaskan malamute. They were regular boarders from the same family, and I always boarded them directly across from one another. Once, when Boo-Boo's mom expressed sadness at having to leave Boo-Boo, I asked her to place the dog at the door to the kennel.

Boo-Boo walked straight down the aisle to her regular pen and flicked the door open with a paw, just wide enough to get in. Because the hinges were mounted on a bias, the pen door closed behind her. Boo-Boo's mom laughed and never again expressed concern about leaving her dogs with me.

Boo-Boo and Nietzsche's parents lived about three-quarters of a mile away as the crow flies and three miles away by road. On one occasion, they scheduled a morning check-in for the dogs before leaving on a trip.

The evening before, I glanced out at my front yard and who should be there but Nietzsche. I put him in a pen and called his dad. I told him Nietzsche was trying to check himself in a day early. He roared with laughter and came to get the dog. Apparently, Nietzsche saw his parents packing, found a way to get loose, and somehow knew where to go.

That is what I mean when I say the best recommendations will come from the dogs themselves. It will generate the kind of word of mouth you can't buy.

In this chapter, we will discuss how to implement the kennel design you've been thinking about. There are a number of things to consider, and I will discuss each topic under its own heading. The first item of business is what the law permits where you are.

Ordinances and Regulations

An easy way to start is with internet searches. Google something like "starting a business in [my town, my county, my province, my state]." The search results for each level of government will give you a starting point.

If you are within city limits, you will need a business license. The department that provides these will be called something like business license division, department of revenue, treasurer, or tax collector. I found it most efficient to gather background information first online, then go to city hall. In person, you may get valuable information in addition to what is online.

While you are there, you'll want to see if noise ordinances apply to your location and whether the city limits the number of dogs you can board. There are areas where you can have only so many pets, and certain breeds are outlawed. There may also be limits on the number of cars unloading and loading or parked at your location.

At city hall, you'll need to check on things like zoning, building codes, and other ordinances. You may need a tax ID number. The city where I now live has a Microenterprise Loan Program for tiny businesses and small businesses. A program like this may be available from your city, county, state, or federal unit of government.

After city hall, I would repeat the same process at the county level. In many places, city hall and the county courthouse are adjacent to each other. Again, I feel more comfortable actually going to the county courthouse to verify online information in person.

Most licenses for a very small business are cheap.

In our state, two other things are required: You must register your business name with the Secretary of State, and you must have a license to board dogs. The supervising authority for the boarding license is the state Department of Agriculture. Information should be available both online and from a local state revenue office.

Our state has 15 different types of animal license based on what you are doing. The licenses cover activities ranging from boarding animals to transporting animals to pet sitting to opening a pet store to starting a rescue shelter. The licenses are inexpensive. Mainly, the state wants to know who is doing what with live animals.

As you see, this process is simply a matter of going to the lowest level of government, then moving up the chain. I was fortunate that I was just outside city limits and everything I wanted to do was permitted by my county. I was also fortunate that neighbors and noise were not a problem. No one lived across the gravel road that ran on one side of my property, and across the two-lane blacktop in front of the house was a pasture.

Your Business Name

There is a book on designing websites, titled *Don't Make Me Think*. That's a principle you want to follow in naming your business. Your business name should make it obvious what you do. That's why the largest pet store chains have names like Petco, PetSmart, and Petsway.

Don't get too clever. You don't want to field calls from people looking for a vet or looking to buy a dog. Those calls are not likely to convert to your business, and the callers will be frustrated they called. That's why I'm not crazy about names like The Happy Hound. It's not clear exactly what the business does.

If you deal exclusively with dogs, the business should have the word dog in it. I was going to do dogs and cats, so I named my business The Pet Hotel. The name also suggests this is a place for a dog that can behave inside, not a place for a dog that runs free or lives on the end of a chain.

An easy formula is: Your location + what the business does. Dallas Doggie Day Care.

Books have subtitles which give additional information about the book. You can do the same by adding a description after your business name, such as "Dog Boarding, Grooming, and Training" or you can add a slogan like "Your dog's home away from home."

Stale? Perhaps. But clear and effective.

Unless your family name is known far and wide and talked about, there is no reason to put your name in the name of your business. The same goes for your farm name or ranch name, unless it suggests something positive. Rolling Acres Dog Boarding suggest spaciousness in a country setting.

At this stage, it helps to search to see if your business name is also available as a website domain name. Sites like GoDaddy and Namecheap can tell you if it is available, and you can use them to purchase the name. Even if you are not sure whether you will have a website, it is smart to buy the name if it is available. If it is not, a small alteration to the name may be. The preferred suffix for a domain name is .com.

Be careful about the implication of the words you use. Hotel means higher price. Motel says bare bones. Chalet, Condo, Dormitory, Hostel, Inn, Guest House,

Lodge, Resort, Spa, and Pet Bed & Breakfast all suggest different things.

Each name indicates a price level and range of activities. You also might want to be careful about using the word Kennel. For some pet owners, it has a negative undertone. To some, it means a breeding facility, not a boarding facility. To others, it might suggest a puppy mill.

If you include a word like Park, which suggests something free and open to the public, you may get unwanted visitors.

Are all the words in your business name easy to spell? Are you using a unique spelling of a word? Can your business name be said easily? All these things can determine how easily you can be found. The name you select is important, and once you have started your business, it will be difficult to change. Put together a list of possible business names and get feedback from family or friends.

Answering the Phone

The first rule for answering the phone is, always have a smile on your face. People will see your smile over the phone.

The second rule is, know what you are going to say. You will need two elevator speeches. An elevator speech is a 30 second commercial or short descriptive statement. When people ask the "tell me something about your business" question, or when they say they would like to board their dog, you must be ready with a prepared response.

The first speech is the one you give for general inquiries. Mine went like this:

"The Pet Hotel is a 24-hour, indoor, pet boarding facility, with heat, air conditioning, exercise yards, music, electronic monitoring, smoke detectors, and fire extinguishers. We are state licensed and inspected, and I live on the premises." Then I would invite callers to come and look around.

Creating it may seem artificial and, in the beginning, saying it will sound canned to your ear, but when you get it down and rattle it off, it conveys authority and helps people trust you. Best of all, everything you say will be true. Keep a copy on a clipboard until you get this speech down pat.

Every time you talk to a client or potential client on the phone, take notes. These notes will often contain valuable information about the caller, their pet, or who recommended your business.

The second elevator speech you need is one that contains the type of pets you accept and what you charge for your services. Before giving this speech, ask the open-ended question, "Tell me about your dog?" The answer to that question will determine if this is a pet you would be willing to provide care for.

Promotion

It's never been easier to spread the word about a business than it is today. The first thing to do is get a free business listing on Google. Google something like "how do I add my business to Google," look over the search results, and follow the steps.

If your business is already in existence, you will probably just need to claim it. If it is a new business, you will need to add it. Google will also let you decide on the category which best describes what your business does.

The more complete your information on Google, the better.

Now is the time to decide on a standard way of presenting your business name, address, and phone number. Will "Street" or "Drive" be abbreviated or spelled out? Will "The" be part of your business name (Dallas Doggie Day Care or The Dallas Doggie Day Care)?

You get the idea. On the internet, on signage, on any brochure or printed material, you always want to use the same standard name, spelling, and way of referring to your business.

The only other search engine I would get a listing on is Bing. There are other places to get listed, many for a fee. I don't consider them to be necessary.

In addition to making your business findable on the internet, you should have a sign. What you use may depend on what is allowed where you are. Where I was, almost anything was permitted. By chance, I met a local artist and helped her with some computer issues. In exchange, she offered to design a logo for me.

The logo she designed was simply perfect. It was a line drawing of a large sitting dog. Nestled within his chest area was a sitting cat. The breeds were not specifically identifiable, but they clearly said dog and cat. It was obvious what The Pet Hotel was: a place to board dogs and cats. (I will get around to cat boarding near the end of this chapter. I promise.)

I painted a two-sided sign with my logo and business name and placed it near the road in front of my house so it could be read from both directions.

You may not know or be an artist, but there's an easy solution. Fiverr.com. This website lists people willing to do artwork and other creative projects for as little as a "fiver." $5. You not only can get a logo designed for a modest fee, but you can also find someone to design your brochure or flyers.

I always had a brochure to give people who stopped by my kennel. I created mine in Microsoft Word. On the front was the logo, business name, address, and phone number. Inside was a description of The Pet Hotel and the services offered.

You can up your online presence by creating a Facebook page for your business. If you already have a personal page, you can add your business on a separate page. You can also, with the owners' permission, include cute pictures of some of the pets that board with you.

Among other things, Facebook is also a huge search engine. People in your area can find you and get your contact information simply by entering something like "dog boarding" and the name of a city. Best of all, Facebook business pages are free.

I would get business cards made. A local print shop can do this for you, or you can buy cards online. You should always have business cards to give out. Business cards are cheap. Give them out freely, even if you are shy, and don't forget to include your email address. The ability to receive email and text messages is expected.

While you are low on clients, here are more things you can do:

Introduce yourself to local vets and groomers and leave business cards. Leave your cards at businesses which have bulletin boards for that purpose. Visit real estate offices, hotels, and motels. They often deal with people who need a place to leave their pet for a few days. Leave cards with them.

If your area has a local paper with low rates, a shopper newspaper, or a radio station with a trading post show, these can also be sources of customers. So can

Craigslist. You can do several newspaper issues in a row when you open, and advertise periodically later. Once you are established, you probably won't advertise near the holidays. That's when you'll have more business than you can handle.

Magnetic signs are available from sign shops and online, and many kennels use them. Placed on your car or truck, they help spread the word. An advantage of these signs is that they are quickly removed in case you go somewhere and don't want to promote your business.

Keep receipts for everything, including gas expenses and car mileage. I always kept my business expenses and receipts in monthly envelopes. Then I segregated the totals by month and added them. These, along with all other income and expense information, went at the end of the year to the woman who did my taxes.

Having a website is important, so important I will discuss websites at greater length in the final section of the book.

In the beginning, you will be worried about attracting business, but actually, a slow start is good. It will help you get your routine down. Avoid opening right before Christmas, when all the other boarding facilities are booked. You could get overwhelmed.

Many of my earliest customers were business owners, doctors and dentists, attorneys and accountants, and members of the local country club. One faithful client was the owner of the local automobile dealership. When dealing with these people or their staff, let them know that you board dogs and let them know how good the care is.

I'm not urging you to be a snob. I'm saying that professional people have money to board their pets, they travel often, and their dogs tend to be well-cared for. They are well-connected in the community. They are the core group that will use your services again and again, and they will get the word out about your business.

Requirements to Board

A daycare collects all kinds of information about parents and their children. Bring them a child who is sick, and they will request that you please take your little one home. If a child acts up, the daycare will call the parents to come get the child.

You will do the same with pet parents and their pets. Like guests in your home, you choose who gets to come to your kennel.

Before accepting any dog or cat for boarding, you will need three things: a completed pet information sheet, a current shot record, and a signed boarding contract.

1. Pet Information Sheet

This is the information you will want on the Pet Information Sheet.

Today's Date
Owner's Name
Address
Phone Number(s)
Emergency Contact
Vet's name and phone number
Pet's name
Age
Sex
Breed

Size or Weight
Spayed or Neutered
Feeding Interval/How much
Special Handling or Health Conditions.

Before you board a dog, or while you are on the phone with the owner the first time, there are questions you may want to ask depending on what the owner tells you.

Where does the dog sleep at night?
Is the dog sensitive to loud noise?
Can you put the dog in a room, close the door, and leave it?

Is the dog food aggressive?
Is the dog aggressive toward people or other dogs?
Has the dog ever bitten anyone?
How often does the dog bark?
Where have you boarded the dog before?

Sometimes you have to suggest to an owner possible problems a dog could have, in order to get them to open up about their pet.

If an owner hesitates about whether their pet is an indoor, housebroken, house pet, if the owner doesn't ask questions about your facility, if the owner wants to board multiple large dogs, or if the owner wants to board one of the breeds you may be concerned about, get additional information. You may decide to turn them down.

It helps to have skill at reading people. If you get a hinky feeling about someone, insist on pre-boarding their pet for a day. If the owner says the dog has never been boarded, ask if the dog is left alone in the house when they are at work. If it has never been left alone, it should be pre-boarded first.

When you pre-board a pet, you will soon know if the dog can stand to be away from the owner. If an owner says, "My dog can't bear to be away from me," this is a dog that can be a problem. Insist on a pre-board. But if the dog has been left with other people or boarded at a vet, chances are it will be okay.

If you ask an owner to preview the kennel and bring the dog for a meet and greet, they will not be able to foist an aggressive dog on you on their way out of town. You don't want to be the kennel for bad dogs. You want to be the kennel for people with well-behaved pets.

You can't believe everything people tell you. Some people are oblivious to how much their dog barks. They simply can't hear it anymore. Some people will deny they have a bad dog because the dog is not bad to them. Remember, the owner needs a place to board their dog, and that might lead them to minimize, forget, or be blind to the flaws of their pet.

When someone puts you in an uncomfortable situation where you need to put your foot down, there is only one solution: put your foot down.

2. Current Shot Record

To board, the following shots should be required:

For dogs: DPP (distemper, parvovirus, parainfluenza), rabies, and bordetella. Canine influenza is recommended, but not required by all facilities.

For cats: FVRCP (feline viral rhinotracheitis, calicivirus, panleukopenia) and rabies.

Most kennels require that vaccinations be given at least 10 days before boarding.

Always keep a copy of each pet's shot record in your files. No pet boards without an up-to-date shot record.

The shot record will either be on a printed form with a grid, or it will look more like a letter. The letter form is given by many vets to pet owners who travel as proof of their pet's vaccinations.

Whatever the form, the shot record should include date of administration and length of time the shot is good for, as well as the name and phone number of the vet. Ask your vet how long it takes for recent shots to take effect, the youngest age at which you should take puppies, and any other local recommendations.

3. Boarding Contract

The boarding contract is an agreement between your business and the owner of the pet. It covers the extent of your liability if something happens to the pet, what the owner is responsible for, and many other issues.

If you board a dog through a site like Rover.com, the booking through them is a contract. You as an independent contractor then fulfill the contract. Nothing more is needed.

If you board a dog through your own business, you need your own contract. Do a Google search for "pet boarding contract" or "pet boarding agreement." Download four contracts from other businesses.

Some of them will read as if written by Ebenezer Scrooge, others are friendly in tone but include all the legal protections you need. I suggest softening the legalese to make yourself sound like the caring person you are, while maintaining the information and protections you need for your business.

Alternatively, if you board a pet with your vet, you can adapt your boarding contract from the one the vet uses.

Have the owner sign two copies of the agreement and take one with them. On the back of my copy of the contract, I always wrote what the dog came with: dog leash, dog collar, one Nylabone, one bag dog food, assorted treats, or whatever.

I've already mentioned the emergency number, but when should it be used? If the pet owners are on their honeymoon, vacationing at Disney World with the kids, or on a cruise, do they need to know the dog is ill or dead? In case something happens, what would they want done? That may be a contingency you want to provide for in your boarding agreement.

When the owner brought their pet, I always gave it the once over for any sign of distress or disease. I would check the groin area for fleas and the ears for ticks. Flea or tick infestation is a reason to reject a dog, or a reason to charge for a bath if you have the ability to bathe dogs.

Who Do I Board?

You can't discriminate against people, but you can discriminate against any type of dog which may be more inherently risky or troublesome than normal. Insurance companies have riders for certain breeds, and rental places have limits on breeds and weights. Your city may have limits.

You can also impose your own limits.

I specialized in small and medium-sized housebroken, house pets, but I didn't discriminate against the Great Dane, Newfoundland, or Great Pyrenees. For the most part, I found the giant breeds easy to handle. And, of course, I had lots of goldens, labs, and mixed breed dogs.

There are numerous advantages to boarding small dogs. In an emergency or with a troublesome small dog, you can wrap the animal in a fresh dry towel, quickly pick it up, and move it where it needs to go. A badly behaving 20-pound dog is nothing like a bad behaving 80-pound dog.

Smaller dogs don't need as much space, so you can do more in a smaller environment. They also don't generate as much waste. If you specialize in housebroken house pets, most of the dogs will be fixed. I never boarded females in heat because that creates additional problems and risks.

I found it helps to have three lists of dogs: Preferred Dogs, Second Tier Dogs, and Refusals. A dog with moderate problems may wind up on your second tier list, which means any Preferred Dog takes priority in boarding when space is tight. I always kept written notes about my refusals.

You are at the beginning of a progression that goes from desperately seeking business to freely turning away people and dogs who don't fit the business model you have created. Along the way you will learn to say, "Sorry, we are not set up to deal with such a strong (people-centered, aggressive, barking, or whatever) dog." Or "I don't think your dog would do well here."

Aggression of any kind towards people creates an obvious right of refusal. This is a service business. It has to work for you, the client's dog, and your other clients.

How can you say no to this nice woman with a troublesome dog? The same way you would say no if she wanted to board a wolf or a bobcat.

Over 90 percent of the owners I dealt with, and their dogs, were no problem. In the early days don't be so desperate for business that you accept a dog beyond your ability to handle. You will pay the price, and perhaps someone's dog will pay the price. If there is a first rule in this business, it's this. You can't board a dog you can't handle or a dog you can't contain.

Is there a risk that two Chihuahuas will kill you or another dog? What about six pit bulls? In the back of your mind, you should be aware of the risk of boarding any particular dog or combination of dogs.

What Will I Charge?

I had only two prices for boarding dogs, one for small dogs and one for large dogs. A small dog was 20 pounds or less. Anything else was a large dog. Once a dog gets past the weight of being easily picked up, it's a big dog. At least to me.

There is not a lot a small dog, up to dickens, can do that picking her up won't solve. A little dog in a kennel cannot wreak the kind of havoc a big dog can. If a little dog growls at you, pick her up with a towel or heavy gloves. A little dog gets muddy or wet, pick her up and wash her in the sink. Even the kitchen sink for a quick cleanup. If the little girl wants to escape, put her in a pet taxi. Problem solved.

But a big dog who decides to have a problem is a whole other ballgame.

Some kennels use three price structures based on weight, some use four, and some use five. The best guide to pricing in your area will probably be found by checking what nearby boarding kennels charge. Set your prices accordingly. If you offer fewer amenities, charge a little less. If you offer more, then charge more.

Based on experience, I have mixed feelings about discounts. You may have to offer discounts based on the market you serve, but I gave discounts only to long-term customers with well-behaved dogs. I would never do it for a stranger or new dog.

What you are selling to your clients is trust. They trust that their pet will be safe and well-cared for. Trust does not come at a discount.

The problem with discounts is this: If you give a discount to anyone, they will tell others, and you will get more and more requests for discounts. The more you give in to discount askers, the more discount askers you will get.

One woman, a doctor, came to look at my facility to make sure it was good enough for her pet. She wanted something special and told me her dog was pampered and needed a lot of care. When she brought the dog in and filled out the boarding contract, she mentioned she was taking a 10-day Caribbean cruise.

Just as she was getting ready to leave, she said, "What kind of discount do you give for a pet staying longer than seven days?

You can think about this a number of ways. Did she want another $50 to spend on piña coladas aboard ship? How much less service a day should I give her dog? Should I give discounts based on the age of the owner? The age of the pet? The length of stay? What?

In the end, I thought it was better to say a simple "Sorry, we do not offer a discount based on time."

When people called on the phone, I always wrote down their name and what they told me. Often they told me far more than the basics.

One man called and mentioned his mom recently retired and didn't want to be burdened with watching his dog anymore while he was out of town. One week later he called to book his pet and asked if I offered a senior discount.

If I had said there was a senior discount, he would have had his mom drop the dog off. Then I wouldn't have had the actual owner's signature on the boarding contract. Luckily, I had this information in the notes I took during his first phone call.

The age of the owner does not change the care the dog will need. Or the fairness of the charge for your labor. The dog will need the same amount of attention either way.

No discounts for length of stay. That was my policy. I made only one exception, and that was for pets that were staying longer than one month. Occasionally there was a pet owner who needed to board a dog for months and months.

For example, one couple ran into a huge construction delay while building their new home. They were forced to move into an apartment that did not allow pets. In a case like this, the dog will become almost like a member of your own family. Set up a schedule for payments and make sure you get a sufficient amount of money upfront.

Check prices in your area. Decide if you want to bill on a per day, per night, or 24-hour basis. You may want a three-day minimum charge over Christmas or other holidays.

You want to keep your pricing streamlined and simple. "One size fits all" pricing isn't possible, but a simple pricing plan will make things so much easier.

Services to Offer

Services you might consider adding include dog walking, daily brushing, doggie day camp, dog training, and extended individual play sessions.

The first service I added to my kennel was bathing dogs. Since I had a full walk-out basement, I was able to walk a dog from the kennel through the exercise yard and into the basement. In the basement was platform I constructed, three feet off the ground, with a regular bathtub. I built a ramp to walk the dog right into the tub. Soft, flexible tubing from the nearest tap, ending in a shower head, allowed me to mix hot and cold water to the perfect temperature.

It doesn't take a great deal of skill to give a dog a bath, but actual full-service grooming is another matter. Becoming a groomer, like becoming a hair stylist, requires training.

If you are interested in becoming a groomer, it may be more convenient to get training before you start your kennel. Once you start boarding, it may be hard to find the time to go to grooming school. However, if you have a business partner, one person could handle the business while the other gets training.

An easy way to start grooming is with your own dog. It comes down to your own judgment and ability to take risk. There are good grooming books available from Amazon and excellent grooming videos on YouTube.

Learning something about grooming, even if you decide not to offer this service, will help you assess prospective boarders. Spotting curled-under nails on a dog, for example, is a sign of a dog that needs more care than he is receiving. An unkempt dog may indicate an unkempt owner. You may not want to deal with either.

If you are interested in learning how to train dogs, owning a kennel gives you plenty of dogs to practice with. When you get some facility as a trainer, this is another service you can offer.

Two organizations which can help you become a trainer are the Certification Council for Professional Dog Trainers and the Association of Pet Dog Trainers.

A final service I offered was funeral arrangements for dogs and cats. I never imagined I'd provide this type of service. It started with a cocker spaniel named Baxter. Baxter boarded regularly for two years. Like some floppy-eared dogs, Baxter's ears were always an absolute disaster—smelly, horrible, and oozing. He always came with multiple meds and always seemed to be in pain.

Finally, his quality of life was so poor his owner asked if I would be the one to take him to the vet and have him put to sleep. She also asked if he could be buried at The Pet Hotel. I buried him outside the fence line under a large oak.

Where I now live, one business specializes in picking up deceased pets from the owner or vet, then either cremating the pet or burying it in their pet cemetery. If the pet is cremated, the ashes are returned to the owner in a cedar box, with the name of the pet engraved on the lid. The lid has a clasp which is secured by a small gold padlock.

In thinking about services to offer, I suggest you don't take on more than you can manage. Start slowly and build from there.

For the services you don't provide, you want to develop a list of recommended resources for pet owners who board their dog with you. This list might include obedience trainers, advanced trainers, good companion animal vets, and professional groomers.

Accounting

A home-based boarding facility is a kitchen table business. Your accounting needs are simple. If you don't already have an accounting system, simply do a search for "envelope accounting system for small business."

In this system, you keep track of your income and expenses in separate envelopes. Invoices and receipts go into different envelopes, usually by month. Items in each envelope are listed on the outside, then totaled each month, quarter, or year.

It's easy to see what you make. It's simply the difference between your income and your expenses. The beauty of the system is that it will teach you basic accounting.

You can also construct your own system using Google Sheets, a powerful spreadsheet program. It's free and Google has tutorials on how to use and design spreadsheets tailored to your own needs.

If you want something more elaborate, do a search for "simple accounting system for small business." Reviews of software will come up. Some of the software is open source, meaning it's free or nearly free, but it will be perfectly adequate for your needs.

An advantage of computer software is that it checks your math. A disadvantage is that it comes with a steeper learning curve and may be more complex than you need.

Kennel accounting software is also available, typically with a recurring monthly charge. It can do everything from scheduling to remembering pet birthdays. But it's too expensive for the beginning home boarder, especially when there are low-cost alternatives with no monthly fees. Kennel accounting software is something to consider only when you have a substantial income.

Remember: you build your business on profit, not expenses.

When accepting payments for boarding, you will need either a receipt book or a quick way to print receipts from your computer.

In the beginning, talk to a bookkeeper or accountant about which records to retain, which deadlines to observe, and which expenses are deductible. For my business I had a local bookkeeper do my taxes. She was highly competent and much more affordable than the local accountants.

The financial advantages of owning a business are hard to quantify but can be substantial in addition to your business income. With a home business, there's no commute, no chipping in for birthdays and baby showers, and no wardrobe expenses.

Pet Waste

The simplest way to dispose of dog feces is to bag it and put it in the trash, where it will go to a licensed solid waste landfill. For a small kennel, that is often a viable solution. That's what I did.

There are also devices that attach to a sewer or septic system and flush the waste there, and there are in-ground dog septic systems. In some areas, there are professionals who specialize in picking up and disposing of pet waste.

The U.S. Department of Agriculture (USDA), through its Natural Resources Conservation Service (NRCS), has at least one publication on Composting Dog Waste, including step-by-step instructions. The end product may be used on plants but is not safe for human consumables.

Their information can be found online by Googling either: USDA + "composting dog waste" or NRCS + "composting dog waste." Some authorities advise against this method, so you have to make your own judgment. The original study was done in Alaska for mushers with many sled dogs. That study advised against composting cat wastes or cat litter for health reasons.

The bottom line on waste disposal is: you must contact local authorities, a public health agency, or a state Environmental Protection Agency to see what is permitted where you live.

Reference Books

People often asked me questions about the characteristics of different breeds. The more I knew, the more it increased my standing with my clients.

When someone brings you a dog, it helps to show the owner you know what breed it is, and if it is a mixed breed, what breeds it appears to favor. When a person asks for suggestions on what breed dog to get, you want to be able to give an authoritative answer based on that person's lifestyle.

I boarded over 45 different breeds on a regular or infrequent basis. Depending on where you live, you will have different breeds that are dominant in your area. Just as there is a variation in individual dog behavior, so there is great variation among breeds. For example, some breeds have a soft mouth while other breeds require caution when giving them treats. Not that they are bad dogs. They are just so exuberant they don't think about your hand, only the treat.

I found it helpful to have two types of reference book, one on dog breeds and one on health and first aid. The ebook versions of these reference books generally don't lay out well on screens. That's why I recommend getting the physical book.

These are not books to read as if cramming for a test in high school. They are books to peruse at your leisure. It's surprising how much knowledge you will pick up without trying.

One word of caution about the breed specific books: Some of these books tell you little more than how wonderful the breed is. The shortcomings of the breed may be ignored or glossed over.

There is an old saying in the dog world that the only thing two dog trainers can agree on is that the third trainer is wrong. Many people have strong opinions. That's why boarding and training advice can be as controversial as talking about politics or religion.

To me, the price of a book is worth it if I get just one good idea. I don't trash authors because I disagree with something they say. I take what I can and am grateful to increase my knowledge.

Don't think you are going to get everything you need in one place. That's like thinking you will get an entire college education from one book.

My advice is to take what you can use, test what you hear, and develop your own best practices.

A general breed book I like is *The Complete Dog Breed Book* by DK (Dorling Kindersley, the publisher). DK also publishes the equally good *The Complete Cat Breed Book*.

The second reference book to have on hand is a book on pet health and first aid. One good book is *The First-Aid Companion for Dogs & Cats* by Amy Shojai. Two other good books are *The Dog Owner's Home Veterinary Handbook* and *The Cat Owner's Home Veterinary Handbook*. Debra Eldridge is the lead author of each.

If boarding is a good business for you, you've probably read many books and can't help reading about dogs.

One thing you might want to check out is the many dog related apps. Apps are simply computer programs that perform a specific function, and Apple, Google, Microsoft, and Amazon among others maintain app stores.

As I write this, there are apps that allow you to do such things as: get advice in real time from a vet; find a pet sitter, dog walker, or dog boarder; get information on a specific dog breed; view and listen to your dog from your phone; obtain dog first-aid information; and plan a walk for your dog.

Beginning Supplies

What you need depends on the nature of your kennel. At a minimum, though, here are some things you will need:

Stainless steel food and water bowls in various sizes
Dog towels to dry dogs
Floor thermometers (the inexpensive kind)
Triple antibiotic ointment for minor scrapes and cuts
First-aid kit
Fire extinguishers
Smoke alarms
Heavy gloves, for handling problem animals
Calculator
Disinfectant for pens
Nightlights for the kennel
Good outdoor lighting
Radio or other sources of music

Indestructible mats for each pen

In addition to the items above, you will want a desk, file cabinet, appointment book or scheduling white-board, and a clipboard or two.

Watch Craigslist for people selling kennel panels, crates, pet taxis, and other supplies. One local farm and home store where we live sells sturdy new pen panels for less than people sell dented, rusty panels on Craigslist. Be aware of new prices so you never overpay for used equipment.

I always had a radio in the kennel so the dogs couldn't hear every outside noise. Find a mellow station. Many of us have an old computer in a closet with an ancient operating system. Adding a couple of external speakers to it can give you a wide choice of music for your kennel from online radio stations.

Each of my pens had an indestructible mat in the back half with food and water bowls in front.

Remote kennel monitoring is a big plus. You can use an intercom system, baby monitor, or web camera. The right web camera system will allow you to monitor the kennel from your desktop, laptop, tablet, or phone.

Rover, RoverGo, and Wag!

With the advent of ride-hailing services like Uber, and short-term rental sites like Airbnb, it was only a matter of time before the peer-to-peer concept would spread to dog boarding.

The basic idea of businesses like Rover and Wag! is to offer pet care services, like dog-walking, siting, and boarding, to dog owners. Rover also offers a program called RoverGo to jumpstart your business.

For those who provide the service, Rover takes 20% of income off the top, RoverGo takes 25%, and Wag Takes 40% (as of this writing).

The pros for becoming a pet sitter or walker this way include:

Gain occasional income
No financial outlay and no investment in a business
Work in a way that fits your own schedule
Gain experience in handling dogs

The cons include:
Low income for the time involved
Too much competition in some areas
Clients may include bargain hunters
Pets may damage your furnishings

These services can provide additional income for people who work at home, students, retirees, and others. They may also provide a first step for those who want to eventually start their own kennel.

From the dog owner's point of view, the quality of care may vary too much, and the pet sitter may not be in business next week, next month, or next year.

Cat Boarding

My basement not only had a walk-out door, but it was also partially above ground and had windows to let in light. It was unfinished, so I added even more lighting and painted the walls white. At one end was my elevated washing station for dogs, at the other end was my cattery. The cattery was arranged so cats could not catch sight of a dog.

I left the basement beams unpainted. They were solid oak beams so old and dry it was almost impossible to drive a nail into them, and they added a rustic element.

The cattery was made of treated lumber in one big unit, almost like a giant closet organizer. Or perhaps you might picture a bookshelf with unusually wide and deep shelving. There were five pens on top, six on the bottom. Each pen was separated by a solid board wall and had a door which took up the entire front.

The whole unit was painted white. The five pens on top contained one double-sized pen for people with multiple cats who wanted them together. It could handle three or more cats. I was able to put one or two cats from the same family in each of the smaller units, depending on the owner's preference.

When finished, the basement cattery was bright and cheerful.

Even if you don't want to board cats, it's not a bad idea to have a few cat pens for people who have dogs and cats. It gives them one place where they can board all their pets, while leaving you free not to take anyone who has just cats.

The alternative for owners who will only be gone a few days is to leave their cat in their house. The owner simply puts out several food stations, sources of water, and litter boxes.

One difference I discovered between dogs and cats is that you can usually teach a dog not to bark, but you can't teach a cat who meows constantly not to do it.

Pinterest, YouTube, and general searches on the internet will lead you to countless plans which can form the basis of your cattery. You don't have to go for deluxe.

As with dog boarding, it pays to ask questions of clients in advance. If someone says they will have to catch the cat, don't take it. That cat may be more wildcat than pet. Ask if the cat yowls when they take it in the car to the vet. If so, be wary.

Cats are harder to confine than dogs, so they must be in escape-proof cages. A dryer vent that opens to the outside may be all a cat needs to flee permanently. Consequently, the building in which you house cats must itself be a secure enclosure before you get to the actual cat enclosure.

The best system is one where the owner puts the cat into the enclosure and retrieves the cat at check-out time. The rest of the time the cage door is closed. This solves one problem you may not have thought about. Sometimes when you open a pen, the cat may attempt an escape.

If you have a small removable or hinged panel on the pen door, you can easily replace food bowls, water bowls, and the litter box without opening the main pen door. You can even add water from the outside using a funnel system.

The oldest cat boarders I had were: a 19-year-old cat who came four to six times a year for several years, and another cat, 22. They were no trouble at all.

Cats don't need much space. They need to be confined and cared for. Food, water, and a litter box is all they need. They don't need what a dog needs. Unlike dogs, they can just chill. Nonetheless, you'll want to go beyond the basics and create a space that allows them to entertain themselves and play.

Don't like cats? Don't do cats. Or specialize in cats. If you don't like to deal with animals outside, cats may be your answer. But you should know that boarding cats does not generate nearly as much money as boarding dogs.

Don't like big dogs or afraid of big dogs? Then from the beginning don't take them. Don't become desperate for business. It's easier to add things as you gain experience than it is to subtract them later.

Now that we've covered what you will need to start your business, a question remains. What is the day-to-day routine in a kennel like?

PART THREE

DAY-TO-DAY OPERATIONS

Morning Routine & Related Ideas

My morning routine began around 7 a.m. I would throw on some clothes and give everyone an out. An early out saves you grief and messes in the kennel because some dogs have owners who are early risers. Before letting out the first dog, I always checked the yard to see if anything had blown in and to chase away any rabbits.

In the darkness of winter, I used a flashlight to check the yard. Even if you live in a city, there can be coyotes, foxes, possums, skunks, raccoons, and other potential problems.

I always mowed the grass outside my fence line very short so nothing could come out of tall grass, weeds, or trees without being seen. I never put a bird feeder near the exercise yard. Feeders attract unwelcome guests, like squirrels and birds. For the same reason, I always fed dogs inside the kennel.

Who got the first out was based on the dog. I looked to see who was dancing the most and gave that dog priority. Then I checked the kennel to see if anyone had an accident. Whenever I handled dogs, I always talked to them by name.

While the dogs were out, I grabbed their food and water dishes, cleaned them, and gave them fresh water.

Some dogs get fed once a day, some twice, and a few three times. I always followed the feeding schedule the owner used. I asked each owner when they boarded their pet to bring the food the dog normally ate. Many owners would have each meal individually packed in sandwich bags.

Boarding can be stressful to a dog, and keeping them on the same feeding schedule with the same food is comforting and helps prevent accidents. Diarrhea is a common symptom of an emotionally upset dog, and a sudden change in food or schedule can trigger it.

One woman brought a Pomeranian to board with me. As usual, I asked her to bring the food the dog ate. She brought sandwich meat, eggs, and other human food.

When an owner feeds something unusual to their dog, they often wait till they drop the dog off before springing it on you. Sandwich meat and eggs was a new one on me, but this dog never ate dog food. Perhaps I should have quoted a higher price on the spot because the food preparation took longer, but I didn't.

Pet food is specially formulated for dogs. There's a danger in feeding dogs people food, especially with the amount of salt and other additives. And some foods like chocolate should never be given. Moist food and human food can be bad for a dog's teeth because dogs can't clean the residue.

However, if you board a dog that is reluctant to eat, it helps to mix a little canned dog food with their regular food. Try it out on a small portion of the dog's food. If they like it, mix in a bit more. For reluctant eaters, I always kept inexpensive cans of dog food on hand.

Most vets use treats to encourage their patients to cooperate. You shouldn't worry about coaxing a reluctant eater either. When asked for an additional service like preparing special food or giving meds, some kennels will add an additional charge for those activities.

Some dogs will not eat if they are being looked at, and some dogs are food aggressive. A dog who growls or guards its food bowl may snap or bite if he thinks his food is threatened.

That's why puppies should get a fair amount of hand feeding, one morsel at a time, to make sure they won't be aggressive about eating. Ideally, you should be able not only to take the bowl from a dog that's eating, you should also be able to put your hand in the bowl. Then the dog should either withdraw or eat around your hand.

A food aggressive dog could bite a child in the face, you in the ankle, or attack another dog if it gets too close. If a dog is food aggressive with its owner, it will be more so with a stranger.

It's easy enough to tell if a dog is food aggressive. With chain link between you and the dog, reach as if reaching for her bowl and watch her reaction. A food aggressive dog will lunge, snap, or growl.

If a dog is food aggressive, there is a workaround. Take the dog out of the pen as if you are going to walk her, put her in an exercise area, go back to the kennel, and put her food in the bowl. Next time when she is out, take the food dish away. Don't let a food aggressive dog see you handle its food bowl.

Remember: it is not your job to cure your client's dog's foibles. You won't have time for that. Just include that information in your records for that dog.

After the dogs were let out and fed, I would go in the house and eat breakfast. I would also check my calendar to see who was coming in or going out today.

Immediately prior to an owner picking up a dog or dropping one off, I would give the kennel a quick spritz with an air freshener. Dogs smell like, well, dogs. Your nose will adjust to the familiar odor, but it may strike a visitor as unpleasant.

After any dog went home, I immediately cleaned and sanitized that pen.

It helps to have an established way for owners to contact you. If you are comfortable with text messages or email, that's fine. But if you would prefer a phone call, especially when confirming drop off or pickup times, make sure the owners know this.

Typically, a dog who got fed in the morning got another out after their meal because feeding and elimination are closely connected in many pets. If I had a dog that was prone to accidents, I would let him out then, too, whether or not he had been fed.

I gave any dog who didn't get fed with the others a plain biscuit or simple dog cookie. Nothing big, just something to stick in their stomach, of a size appropriate to the dog.

High energy dogs like Bob and Max, the Dalmatian and lab, need to be let out more often. Youngsters need to be let out more than oldsters, and watching water level is important. If a dog guzzles water, it requires more outs.

When giving dogs outs, I wanted to disperse urine uniformly throughout the yard. To do this, I alternated using the main exercise yard with the 10 x 10 enclosures. During or after every out I did a poop patrol, and I watered the areas where the dogs peed the most to wash urine from the grass.

It all becomes rote, like farmers with cows. You set up a routine that works for you and works for the dogs.

In the early days of establishing your kennel, when you are trying to win the confidence of owners, you don't want things that may put off potential clients. When you present the kennel to a new person, the grounds should be kempt and the dog facilities clean.

Potential clients visiting your facility for the first time feel like they are hiring a babysitter they don't know. They want reassurance.

Later, when they know your operation, they will sign a boarding agreement, hand you the dog's leash, and drive away without a second thought. If you maintain your kennel so anyone who drops by will like what they see, it will not only please your clients, you should never have a problem with a state inspector.

We can never forget the emotional attachment owners have to their dogs, though we may never know exactly how deep that attachment is. That's why you want to provide the best care you reasonably can.

One client, a man, often brought me a Boston terrier to board. After two years of regular boarding, he explained what the dog meant to him. The dog had been his daughter's, a 17-year-old high school student. One snowy morning she was driving to school, lost control of her car on a curve, and hit a tree. She died. That little terrier was his last living link to his daughter.

Midmornings I let everyone out for exercise. You can have indestructible yard toys that everyone can play with, like Kongs, which you can clean later. With dogs that fetch, you can play toss to get them to run around. In warm weather, I had a wading pool the dogs could play in, and I let them air dry.

Your morning routine will vary according to the dogs you have. For example, if someone brings a lab and a huskie and two other people bring a golden and a mix, and the dogs get along, let them play. While watching over them, you can post on Facebook. A lot of your guests will become regulars, so it helps to keep a record of how each dog behaves with other dogs.

Some dogs won't come when called. For example, Toby, the Akita I mentioned earlier, loved to be outside but he didn't like to be called back to the kennel. When Akitas are puppies, they look like baby lambs with upright perky ears. They don't look real. They look like the most amazing plushy toy ever. They are like snuggling up to 10 pounds of pure joy.

But when they are full grown, they are 110 pounds of pure power. They look at you with eyes that seem to say, "I know what you are thinking," and they show pearly teeth all the way to the back of their jaw. Without training, they can be just on the edge of being dangerous.

So when it was time for Toby to come in, I never demanded that he come in or threw a leash on him. I'd show him a Pup-Peroni and head quickly to the kennel. Now we were playing a game. At the door of the kennel, I gave him one treat and dropped the second Pup-Peroni in his pen. Then I closed the pen door and said: "You are such a good boy," in the most theatrical way.

He was happy, and I was happy. If you've ever seen a greased pig contest on YouTube, you have an idea what it's like to get an Akita into a pen when he doesn't want to go. If people weren't smarter than dogs, it would have been a battle of wills and strength and Toby would have won.

In general, you don't get angry with a dog. It serves no purpose. You figure out why the dog acts as it does and use its nature to get it to do what you want. Books on dog behavior can be invaluable in refining your methods of kennel management.

Before lunch and again in the early evening, I worked with any dog in for training. I kept training sessions short and fun.

If you think about the number of outs a dog with a working owner gets, you can see the advantage to the dog owner of this type of boarding kennel. A dog will get many more outs and more exercise and attention.

Outs also depend on the weather. If it was 100 degrees Fahrenheit, the dogs got short outs, and I made extra sure to check water levels. Sometimes I would drop an ice cube in the water bowl to cool it without making it cold. Some dogs really enjoyed this. Others decided to play in the water.

I always kept an eye on the weather forecast and radar so I could modify the out schedule when rain was likely. Even a brief break in the rain can give your boarders a chance to get in and out safely.

Midmornings were also a good time to catch up on paperwork, make photocopies, or make notes on the dogs in the kennel. It's a good time to work on advertising, post to Facebook, or add something to Pinterest or Reddit. Depending on temperature, you can do many of these things while outside with the dogs.

It goes without saying that I always kept my phone with me and a clipboard or notepad nearby. Always be prepared for calls, even when you are in the grocery store.

Not every day will you have someone preview the kennel. Not every day will you have a dog to wash. But there will almost always be inquiries and scheduling calls.

Let me conclude this chapter by saying there would be no point in writing this book if I didn't tell you the truth. The truth includes the mistakes I made. Some of those mistakes, the big ones, will be found in the next two chapters.

Noon Routine & Assorted Facts

Sumi (pronounced "sue me") was an older Shar Pei. Docile and quiet, she would rather be left alone. She had stayed at least a dozen times before it happened, and her stays were never longer than a weekend. Her owners had not previously told me about any aggression on her part, and I always handled her like the grumpy old girl she was. Shar Peis have short tails, but her tail never moved and never wagged, not even with her parents.

Sumi never came when called. I was lucky to get her to even acknowledge me. She would come out of the kennel fine on her own. She would eat and drink like any other dog. But to get her to go back into the kennel, I always had to go get her. I would approach her from the front, say "Sumi, let's go," and snap a lead on her.

The "thing" about Sumi was a peculiar movement she did, difficult to describe. It was an unusual sort of motion she'd make with her head and neck, like she was sneaking a look at you and trying to see if you were watching her. It was a little unnerving. For that reason, I always wore gloves when I handled her.

Some dogs are not extraverts, but most dogs are. They like people. But not Sumi.

One day Sumi is in the yard, as far from the kennel as she can get. I go over to her because it's time to lead her back to the kennel. I do not have my gloves on. From the side, I start to reach for her collar with my left hand. In my right hand, I have the leash. As I reach for her collar, she does the "thing."

Then Sumi bit me.

Right before the bite, I got a flash. It wasn't my life flashing before my eyes, but I got a flash of something. As I reached for her barehanded, her head started to move. I thought, "Damn, I don't have my gloves on." Before I could start to pull back, she had me.

I know I made a sound. I don't know what sound I made, but she immediately released. I am not a screamer, so I think it was probably just an exhale of air.

I told Sumi it was okay, went back to the kennel, got the gloves, clipped a lead on her, and put her away. Then I tended to my hand. In the area between the thumb and index finger, she pierced the skin top and bottom. She pierced the flesh on both sides though not all the way through.

It never really hurt. I cleaned the wounds and took an ibuprofen. Then I called her vet to make absolutely sure she was up to date on her shots and to tell them that she bit me, just so they knew. I let them know she released right away.

I didn't blame her. I knew she was a cranky old girl, and she wasn't happy coming to the kennel. I should have had my gloves on, and I didn't. I am not sure I talked to her before I reached for her.

She was the only dog who ever bit me.

Handling some dogs is like riding a horse. You turn in the saddle, and the horse can feel a change in the position of your ass. The horse can react to a change you aren't aware of. A cranky horse can tell the person on their back isn't paying attention and might think, "I will flick her off." Or it could simply be the horse thinks, "This isn't right, I'm scared," and off goes the rider.

With Sumi, I was not driving the horse. I am aboard the horse, but I am not on board the horse. My mind is elsewhere. How nervous do you get when the driver of the car is looking too much at you and not enough at the road? That's what this is like. When you handle animals, you need to keep your eyes on the road.

Later I realized Sumi was losing her eyesight. Her reaction was probably nothing more than self-protection. If I had approached directly in front, if I had said her name, it wouldn't have happened. It wouldn't have happened if I had been on board.

Sumi (sue me) may not be the best name for a dog that bites, but the point is, when you are with a dog, be with them. You can't be thinking about something else. A dog that's ill or debilitated can act contrary to its usual nature. The same goes for a dog out of its usual situation.

With dogs I rarely used gloves. It was seldom necessary. After you are around dogs long enough, you can look at some dogs and sense if you need to be wary. You may not know why the hairs on the back of your neck are standing up, but you know something is amiss.

Sumi's odd head motion wasn't a flash. It was a slow look down and then a slow look in the other direction. But the first time I saw it I knew I had to use gloves on her. She didn't bare her teeth, snap at me, or growl. None of that. She never barked. What I instinctively saw in her proved true.

I am not scared of dogs. Had I had my gloves on, I would have been tagged but not hurt. In fact, if I had my gloves on, the gloves would have been a signal to walk in front of her, talk to her, then reach for her.

With dogs, you always have to be the alpha. You have to be the dominant one. You can't set yourself up for them to challenge you and then have to back down. The human is always the boss. Dogs never get the upper hand. That has to be the rule in your kennel.

There's a reason dog shows have dogs in different classes. The different breeds are different. Familiarity with groups and individual breeds will make understanding canine behavior easier. In addition, dogs within each breed are different from one another and dogs differ by the way their owner raised them.

One woman, Debbie, always brought three dogs to board: a Pomeranian, a spaniel, and a Shar Pei mix. The latter two were her dogs, and they were well-behaved. The Pomeranian was her mom's dog, and it growled and snapped. It had classic small dog syndrome, meaning it showed uncorrected, dominant behavior toward people. She was fine if you didn't touch her and she didn't bother other dogs, but she was not a friendly dog.

My golden retriever Einstein always followed me around. A dog I have now, Gunther, is a Rottweiler, a herding breed. He wants to take the lead. Gunther is like the backseat driver who doesn't know where you are going but wants to tell you how to get there. He's not aggressive; he simply wants to herd something.

Gunther is a young dog. He is the worst he will ever be. Last month he was the worst he will ever be. The month before he was the worst he will ever be. A young dog with a good owner only goes one direction. They keep getting better and better and better as they get older. In addition, a young dog like Gunther needs much more activity than an older dog, though some older dogs are also goers.

Another dog I have now, Riley, is a Shih Tzu mix. She's five years old. Dogs over five are reasonably relaxed about boarding. Riley is a small dog, and dogs mature in different ways by size. Large breeds take longer to mature.

There are also sex differences in dogs. Males, especially ones that are not fixed, will try to mark. When you walk a male dog into the kennel, lightning fast, he may lift a leg and pee into the pen of another dog. That's why, when a male is first dropped off, you can calm him down by giving him an out before going into the kennel. He will often pee himself out as soon as he smells the other dogs.

Sporting dogs, scent hounds, sight hounds, terriers, herding dogs, working dogs, toy dogs are all different.

Learning general patterns and individual behaviors will help you immensely.

At lunch time in the kennel, I fed anyone who needed to be fed, though it's a rare dog who needs a midday feeding. After lunch, I would do another round of outs. If anyone had paid for grooming, nail trims, extra brushing, or a bath, I might do that while the other dogs had an afternoon siesta.

Tables in restaurants are numbered even though the numbers aren't usually visible to the patrons. You may want to do the same with dog pens for convenience in scheduling.

Some people use a white board and erasable marker, some people use a reservation book, some people use a spreadsheet or other software. However you do it, if you number your pens, it can help you keep track of who goes where within the available boarding space.

I used blank calendar sheets with headings that let me fill in the date and which dog would be in a particular pen. If the dog was boarding for multiple days in a row, I simply extended the line to the last date. I always kept the old sheets. That gave me a snapshot of the busiest times in the year. It also gave me an idea when to advertise, though after my first year I did a little advertising.

I mentioned before there was a breezeway between the house and the kennel. In the breezeway was a short white wooden fence with a latched gate on a spring. It was a convenient place to meet clients and let their dogs into the kennel. On the gate, I posted a sign that read: Do Not Open.

One day a meter reader came to read the electric meter. He knew what my business was, and he knew it was easier to read the meter from the gravel road behind the kennel. Still, he let himself in the gate, ignoring the sign. I think he was just being a bit nosy.

By chance, I was on the deck overlooking the exercise area. With me was one of my long-term boarders, a 120 pound Rottweiler named Sentry. When the dog saw the meter reader appear unexpectedly, he went on full alert, hackles up, a deep growl in his throat. The meter reader stopped in his tracks.

Call me a naughty person, but I couldn't help myself. I stayed on the deck with Sentry and let the meter reader stew for a minute before calming the dog.

I'll admit I was more than a bit ticked off. This man ignored the sign and opened the gate even though he knew I might be working with dogs off lead. But I learned an important lesson. People don't pay attention to signs. The people you most want to follow the warnings on a sign are often the people least likely to do so.

After this incident, I made sure all external gates had a chain and padlock, with the same key opening each lock. The default position for each gate was locked.

Put up signs on your property if you feel like it. Just don't trust that they will always work. What works is creating barriers that can't be bypassed.

Let me say a word about people when they drop off dogs. You might have a mom showing up with three small children and two dogs. Her kids think your kennel is a petting zoo. They will try to reach in to pet dogs that are unfamiliar with children, afraid of children, or perhaps don't like children. And mom may be oblivious or blasé, not giving a thought about the potential risk the dog may pose.

If you allow kids in the kennel, there will be huge tearful goodbyes, their dog will get overwrought, and it will rile up the other dogs, too. The simple solution is to take the dog into the kennel yourself.

On holidays, all the vets will be booked. If they have any space left, it will be reserved for sick or injured animals. There will be no backup place to take a dog you can't control. For that reason, you want to reserve holidays, especially Christmas, for your tried and true customers, dogs you know, and dogs you have preboarded.

Over Christmas and other holidays, you want to make maximum use of your space. If someone wants to book a dog for a day, you may have to waitlist them, charge them for more days than they board, or not take them at all. You don't want to turn away a dog that will book for a week in the same spot.

With an agreeable dog from a good owner, you can even take the dog into your home if it gets along with your dogs. Do people take that as unprofessional? No, they think it makes them and their pet special. They will be thrilled.

In general, on holidays you book your preferred people and preferred dogs first. A couple of months before the holidays, call your best customers and say, "The Pet Hotel will have enough guests that I will be forced to turn away some dogs or cats. You are such a good client I want to call you now to lock in your spot if you are going to need one."

Then check back with them as you get closer to the holiday.

If an owner says, "The dog won't listen to anybody but me," don't board the dog. That dog gets to go with the family on vacation. If an owner says, "We will bring the cat in if we can catch him," don't board that cat.

Do not give in to an owner's desperation. Suggest that a friend or family member come to their house to care for the animal. Last minute begging, "I'll pay you extra. Please, please, please?" should always get the same answer for a dog you don't know. No.

If you cannot say no, this is not the right business for you. I learned the hard way to be immune to sob stories.

A few weeks before Christmas one year, a military family called and said they had to go home for a quasi-emergency and wanted to stay for the holiday. The husband explained that they had four German shepherds. Outside dogs, he said, but well-behaved.

I agreed to take them.

I had a portable pen on a concrete slab, complete with roof and shelter. The pen was six feet high, and that's where I thought I would put the shepherds. When the man arrived in an SUV with the dogs, they were unruly, but I thought they were just excited. Still, something gnawed at me. The dogs seemed a bit too wild.

Once the owner left, things got worse. The four shepherds were determined to leave. The largest of the dogs was the ringleader, and he made repeated attempts to scale the sides of the enclosure. After three hours, I had no choice. I called the soldier, explained what was happening, and told him to come get his dogs. The four shepherds were doing everything possible to escape.

Half an hour later, he showed up in a small sedan with three buddies. The car was so small he said he could only take one of the dogs, the ringleader. As he led the dog to the car, he remarked, "This dog will go through a plate glass window to get to me." Then he gave me a scary sort of grin and left.

I thought about the situation for sixty seconds. Then I called his wife and demanded the removal of the other three howling shepherds. An hour later, the dogs were gone. As the man left this time, he said with a smirk, "I am the only one who can handle these dogs."

Four uncontrollable dogs for five hours. What a mess! But it reinforced what I already knew. First, when in doubt, pre-board. Second, don't give in to sob stories. And third, be cautious about three or more large dogs from the same owner. That's a pack, and a pack behaves differently than an individual dog.

A problem with boarding German shepherds is their popularity. It goes all the way back to World War I when an American soldier rescued one of the breed in France. That dog and its heirs appeared in dozens of movies and a TV series under the name *Rin Tin Tin*. German shepherds have also been continually glamorized through their use by police and the military.

As any breed gains in popularity, it becomes profitable for careless breeders to produce more and more poorly bred dogs. The result, at least in my area, is that many German shepherds are nervous, excitable dogs, prone to separation anxiety. When I heard the words "spoiled" and "German shepherd" in the same sentence, I came to regard it as a no-board.

Dalmatians suffer from popularity in a somewhat different way. The Dalmatian has a history as the official mascot of firehouses. In the days of horse-drawn fire wagons, the dogs would run ahead of the fire engine, barking for people and carriages to get out of the way.

The 1950s novel *The Hundred and One Dalmatians* spawned a Disney movie and many sequels and spinoffs. As a result, the dogs gained instant popularity. The Dalmatian problem is they are high energy dogs. Many people select a dog based on its looks or popularity rather than based on a thoughtful consideration of their own lifestyle.

That was the case with one woman who came to me to board her dog. She and her husband, a doctor, grew up without dogs, but they thought having a dog would be good for their son. Though they lived in a subdivision and had only limited time to give a dog, they got a border collie.

Border collies are true working dogs. We have friends who manage cattle from horseback with the help of trained border collies. These dogs are whip-smart and extremely high energy. Without stimulation and work, they get bored silly and can become neurotic and destructive.

This couple's problem, a poor match between dog and owner, is a problem you will see in your kennel.

Kennel management is something I figured out as I went along. As I mentioned, in the winter, if I only had a few dogs, I kept the heat low and put the dogs in pens nearest the radiant electric heater. When the kennel was fuller, I used the ceiling fan to evenly distribute the heat and keep the front pens from getting too warm.

Year round I used two or three floor thermometers to monitor temperature at dog level throughout the kennel. I did the same thing for the cats. Floor thermometers are an essential.

When the kennel was not busy, I put all the dogs in larger pens because they were easier to clean. With the AC on, the last pen I filled was the one directly under the air conditioner. I kept a board to place over the back half of that pen to keep cool air from dropping straight down on the dog.

Part of kennel management is handling demanding owners, the kind of people who want you to walk their dog eight times a day, brush her, and hand feed her. Let them know with each demand that it costs more. Say, "That's extra."

Poker players talk about "tells." A player with a tell struggles to suppress a smile when he has a good hand, while the same player with a bad hand might furrow his brow. Something similar happens with bad pet owners. They all sound alike. Once you hear their phrasing three or four times, you will learn to avoid dealing with them and their dogs.

In normal procedure, an owner calls and you talk about the kennel and their dog. Then they come to the kennel and bring the dog, if you ask. If they say it is too much trouble, simply tell them it is required. It should not be trouble to bring a well-behaved dog someone cares about to preview the kennel.

A person with a problem dog will not want you to pre-see that dog. There are dogs a seven-foot fence won't defeat. There are dogs that are like dealing with a lion. You can't touch it, you can't handle it, you can't contain it. There are dogs, especially in rural areas, who are as free to go anywhere as a person. The dog may be linked to their owner, but they are essentially autonomous beings.

This is not to scare you out of starting a kennel. This is to make sure, when you start your boarding kennel, you won't get into bad situations. Indoor, housebroken, house dogs are the easiest dogs to begin with. Later, when you want to expand, you may decide to take other dogs or add an indoor/outdoor kennel with runs for outdoor dogs.

One limitation of this business is that it is a seven-day-a-week proposition. Some people are fine with that. But if you need to schedule time off, say two weeks in the spring, be sure to tell your regulars well in advance. The best time for me to take time off was during the first three months of the year. It was always my slowest time.

The day-to-day work in a kennel is not continuous. There are hours-long gaps throughout the day when nothing needs to be done.

I never waitressed or cashiered. Aside from babysitting when I was a kid, I never had a job where I took money directly from a customer. So operating a boarding kennel was a first for me in that way as well.

When you start, you may want to accept only cash or checks. Or you may want to check out PayPal or credit card options. Just be careful not to be trapped by high credit card processing fees and always add those processing fees into your pricing.

As a reminder, on holidays you will be very busy, and that is why you want only the crème de la crème. I was not afraid of dogs, and in some ways that led me to take those four German shepherds.

You can't be sorry for people. Who will feel sorry for you when you board a dog you can't hold, or who will hurt you, or who will escape? That's why socializing a dog when it is young, taking it places, and letting it be around other people and dogs is so important.

I learned the hard way to ask questions when someone called the first time. "Where does the dog sleep 95% of the time?" is a good question to ask. One man told me his dog was housebroken and slept in the kitchen. When he returned to pick up his dog, I told him the dog messed repeatedly in the kennel.

Then he told me the full story. The dog did sleep in the kitchen but only in severe thunderstorms. Technically the man didn't lie, but some people will break the spirit of what you are asking them. All they are thinking is, "I've got to go somewhere, and someone has to watch my dog." Sleeping indoors in a storm does not make a pet a housebroken, house dog.

That's why sensitivity to noise is a good question to ask. Thunderstorms involve changes in pressure, low and high-frequency noise, and a sudden burst of intense light. Some dogs need medication to cope with that, and depending on where you live, the Fourth of July may be as bad for a dog as a thunderstorm.

Chewers pose a different kind of problem. How can a dog that has something to chew on every day spend a few days in the kennel with nothing to chew on? That's why it's a good idea to ask the owner if their dog is a chewer. If they are, ask the owner to bring one of the dog's non-destructible toys from home.

Never leave a dog alone with a new toy. It should be something the dog has been tested on. Even then you want to monitor how the dog uses the toy and decide how long to leave the toy with the dog.

When you are fooled by what an owner tells you, mark the dog down on your do-not-board list. If the owner presses you, simply tell them their dog is not a good fit. Or you can say he's not happy here, he mopes, he doesn't take boarding well, he doesn't eat, or he cares so much about you that you should think about a house sitter.

You may think I am being harsh or judging people. But it's just another application of the 90/10 rule. Ten percent of the people will cause 90 percent of your problems. Don't board the dogs of those 10 percent and your problems will be mild.

There is no room for a problem dog in your kennel. People can raise a dog however they want. They can prevent it from being a good citizen. That's their choice. But they don't get to make their choice your problem.

In a boarding situation where clients can see many or all of the dogs, some people will be nervous seeing any of the breeds with a bad reputation. It will lose you business. In the same way, you don't want aggressive dogs in the kennel. You don't want to be showing the facility and have a dog snapping or growling.

At the end of each spring teenage girls would show up at the kennel looking for a summer job. I never accepted their offers. First, I was really efficient and could still manage on my own. Second, and the main reason, I didn't want the liability. "Family only" simplifies your life until you get really big.

Boarding dogs you will meet a wide range of people. One of my clients was a famous nonfiction author whose articles appeared in newspapers and in magazines like The New Yorker. At least one of her books was a New York Times bestseller. But when she first came, she appeared at my front door dressed like an old man farmer: overalls, floppy hat, gray hair, old boots.

Her dog was mostly shepherd and totally agreeable. The first time she boarded, I was on the phone and didn't catch her last name. Her signature was a bit of a scrawl, and it didn't register. Another time I made her take her dog to a groomer because it came covered in fleas and ticks. Only later did I realize who she was.

I never had a dog abandoned with me. Abandonment can be a problem when you operate a kennel. Someone drops off a dog with you and never comes back. That's one reason why you want to get most or all of your money upfront, except with trustworthy clients, and why you only want well-cared-for dogs, the kind that won't be deserted

Twice people abandoned a dog in my front yard. Each time it was the familiar "drive in the country and dump the dog" scenario. In each case, the dog ran off before I could corral it.

People will say all kinds of crazy things to you. Things like, "My dog is only a year old. That's why he doesn't have all his shots yet." Maybe the people who say that actually believe it. Who knows? But people who aren't bright enough to get their dog shots are not bright enough for you to deal with.

Sometimes there will be heartbreaking stories. Against my normal practice, I once boarded a seven-week-old puppy in a true emergency. He was a yellow lab, large for his age, and I isolated him to minimize exposure to other dogs. He was actually too young to have had all his shots, but I reasoned the only dogs who would be susceptible were other puppies. At the time, all the dogs in the kennel were adults with up-to-date shot records.

The yellow lab was there two nights and gone the morning of the third day. This puppy peed once on the floor. I told him no, and he was housebroken. He learned Sit on the first repetition. I taught him other simple tricks that he also learned in one try.

When the owner came to pick him up, I told her he was the brightest young lab I had ever seen. I found out later she had him living at the end of chain, where he was teased by kids playing basketball in their driveway.

When her husband went to calm the dog, the dog bit him. She called me and asked if the dog bite could be a medical problem for her husband. I asked about the dog's vaccinations. The dog was more than a year old now, and she informed me that he hadn't had any shots because "he's still too young for that."

These were educated people with a nice home in the country. Middle class or upper middle class. The dog's name was Buddy, but they sure didn't treat him like a buddy. This was a genius dog, and his owners kept him chained!

The Buddy story was a bad experience, but I saved my worst experience for the next section.

Night Routine & Final Thoughts

In the late afternoon, I fed each dog and gave them another out. If I had a dog for training, I would do a second training session in the early evening.

At bedtime, each dog received a final out, and I checked on each dog's condition. Medication was dispensed if needed. Each dog got a good word and a little something to put in his stomach before he went to sleep. I double-checked the temperature to make sure it was right for the night.

The main lights in the kennel went off, and the only light was from a soft nightlight. The radio played quietly on. I double checked that all gates were closed and all locks locked.

Many times I was called in the night by one of my regular clients with a death in the family or other emergency. "Can we bring her over now?" they would ask. I always told them, "I'll meet you at the front door."

If you are just starting out, you don't want to get discouraged by having something bad happen right out of the gate. You want to do things in a way that will help build your self-confidence.

The experience that most rattled my confidence involved two Chihuahuas, Jack and Zoe, from the same owner. Jack was a white Chihuahua, about five pounds, built like a can of Dinty Moore stew. When Jack was in the exercise area, I always followed him around because he was not only ancient, he was blind.

His companion, Zoe, was a longhaired Chihuahua, scarcely over two pounds. Zoe was fawn colored, a light brown mixed with a dusky brown like fall colors. She was an exceptionally shy dog, one of those dogs who doesn't run to you or respond to her name. The dogs were so small you could pick them up at the same time.

At The Pet Hotel, most trees were oaks whose leaves ran to brown in autumn. It was early fall and Zoe and Jack were in the exercise yard. The sun was starting to set. As usual, I was following Jack. I turned my back on Zoe for a minute, and she was gone.

I felt a twinge and scanned the yard again. I looked outside the fence line. She wasn't there. Then my brain kicked in, and I had an idea. I put Jack in the kennel and went into the house to get Einstein, my golden retriever. I gave him Zoe's blanket to smell, left him off lead, and together we went outside the fence. Einstein headed right for the blacktop road in front of the house.

I did not believe him. It was far more likely the dog would go to the big field down from the fence. I called Einstein back. Since it was getting dark, I left him in the yard and got a flashlight to search the field. She wasn't there.

I called Zoe's family. Her owners were gone, but I reached their young adult children and told them Zoe was missing. I also called area vets and the police. Then I lined the outside of the fence with pet taxis and put food and water bowls next to each one. The night was already getting chilly. If Zoe came back during the night, at least she would have shelter, food, and water.

That night I didn't sleep. Dread alternated with panic.

First thing the next morning, I called the local radio station and asked them to make repeated announcements about the lost dog. I gave them Zoe's description and offered a reward. I asked them to tell listeners that she doesn't like to be picked up and will bare her teeth, but she won't bite, and she can be picked up.

After calling the radio station, a relative of the owner arrived and helped me search the wooded area beyond my field. Again, no luck. By midmorning, Zoe's mom returned to town and came to retrieve Jack. I told her everything I was trying. She was calmer than I was.

Then at noon, I got a phone call.

A couple with a child, driving on the highway, heard the radio ad and saw Zoe walking along the ditch. They scooped her up and called the radio station. The receptionist gave them my number, then they called me. The description they gave over the phone was perfect. I gave them directions and called Zoe's family to tell them she had been found.

Zoe had been gone 16 hours and travelled less than a mile. When the couple who found the dog arrived, I thanked them and gave them their reward. When Zoe's mom picked the dog up, she brought me flowers.

The two dogs often visited afterward, but each time I kept a close eye on them and Zoe went out with her little leash on. For the next several years I would sometimes wake up in the middle of the night brimming with anxiety, imagining Zoe was gone.

I can tell you what Zoe did. She found a spot in the chain-link fence that a two-pound dog could wiggle through. This teeny-weeny, little-bitty, minuscule, hardly bigger than a baseball, dog. She went through the fence into the ditch alongside the county road in front of the house and followed it a third of a mile to the highway. Then she turned right, staying in the contour of the same ditch.

It was the path of least resistance. Zoe couldn't get through high grass, and the rain-scoured ditch kept her off the road and away from vehicles.

If I had listened to Einstein, she wouldn't have gotten far. Einstein would have found her. But at the time I was too panicky to do one thing for more than a minute because there were so many things to try. I had 360 degrees to search, Zoe was the color of the fall leaves, and the path she took, toward traffic, was the path I least expected.

No one ever escaped again.

If there is one lesson I learned, it is this: be careful when dealing with exceptions to the rule. These two dogs were the smallest I ever had stay at the kennel.

The next lightest dog was 10 pounds, five times Zoe's weight and twice the size of Jack.

I had a bad experience of a different kind with a male miniature schnauzer I boarded many times. He was about 20 pounds, nicely groomed, a pale gray, almost silvery. He was off his feed when he was checked in, and that was really unlike him. He was lethargic where normally he would be active and responsive.

The next morning I called his owner, who was out of town, and told her I wanted to take the dog to the vet. She agreed. The vet examined him and decided to keep him. The following day the vet told me the dog died. She asked if she could do a necropsy, which is what an autopsy for animals is called. I called the owner and got permission.

It turned out the little schnauzer died from a perforated diaphragm. Only after I told the owner about the results of the necropsy did she tell me her nephew had kicked the dog the day before. The dog seemed all right to her at the time, she said, though she confessed she had a nagging feeling something was wrong.

If Zoe escaped the first month I was in business, if the four shepherds came in those first few months, or if early on someone dropped off a dog that died in my kennel, that would have been the end of the kennel. But I had the kennel for years before anything bad happened.

Part of this was because my volume of business was lower in the beginning, and as business increases, there is a greater probability something bad will happen. Yet at the same time, as your business grows, you gain more skill in handling situations.

As your skill grows, you learn more about the eccentricities of dogs. Some are afraid of men, cats, hats, brooms, or something else. Some dogs have sensitive spots, like a tail you better not touch. Some dogs will gnaw on anything.

There are dogs that will grab a piece of chain-link fence and bend it back and forth until it breaks. One old basset hound I boarded had gums in such poor condition he dislodged two teeth gnawing on a section of chain-link.

Dogs who gnaw can often be discouraged by spraying the object of their attention with a bitter apple spray. But some dogs, like the basset hound, require constant vigilance. That's why it's helpful to have one or two extra secure pens.

If I were starting over, I would have two pens with a door made of the same corrugated metal as the kennel walls. This would allow for light and air circulation from above while at the same time giving the dog no chewable surface.

Nothing can prepare you for every possible eventuality. I am not naturally suspicious or naturally unsuspicious. I am situationally suspicious. When the hair stands up on my arm, I look around and see what's causing it.

But when a long-haul trucker brought me a Rottweiler that was skin and bones, I was instantly in sympathy with the dog. A friend, he said, was supposed to feed the dog, but when he got off the road, the dog was like this. Emaciated. The trucker brought no food even though that was part of our conversation when I talked to him on the phone.

I thought his story was plausible, and when he said, "I got to get back on the road or I will lose my job," I agreed to take the dog. One thing struck me as odd. The dog was named Freddy Krueger, after the serial killer in *A Nightmare on Elm Street*.

But the dog needed care, and Krueger had a rabies tag on his collar, so I knew which vet to call.

After the trucker had left, I realized the dog could not stay on his feet. I carried Krueger into the house and let him lie on the kitchen floor. He looked like he might die. It was night. I called a vet who came to the house. He figured the dog weighed 50 or 55 pounds and should have weighed twice that.

The vet gave Krueger a perfunctory farm-dog examination and said he thought the dog's kidneys were shutting down. His only recommendation? Put him down.

"I can do it here," he said.

"He just got here," I said. "He's not my dog. I can't put him down."

I spread newspapers on the kitchen floor and rolled Krueger onto blankets so I could slide him around. Then I soaked dry dog food in water and fed him one piece at a time by hand.

He stayed in the kitchen three weeks. At first, I had to flip him over because he couldn't turn from one side to the other. He wasn't just emaciated; he was dehydrated. After a few days, he was able to lift his head up, and I was able to put a bowl under his face.

Slowly he got better.

In the beginning, Krueger peed and pooped on the newspaper, and I cleaned up after him. There were only a few days of that, then I moved him on a rug to the front door and helped him to his feet so he could go outside to pee.

Every once in a while the trucker would call me from the road and say, "I'm really mad at the guy who did this." At one point he stopped in to see the dog and put more money down on the bill. After a few months, he came and took the dog.

Nine months later the trucker brought Krueger back for boarding. There was no resemblance to the dog who first came to the kennel. He had fully recovered. But there was one thing wrong. The dog had dried blood on his head above his eyes. "The dog ran into something," the man told me.

Days later I got a call from a woman who introduced herself as the trucker's ex-wife. She asked if I had Freddy Krueger. When I said I did, she asked if she could come over. Half an hour later she arrived with her little girl.

The ex-wife had quite a different story to tell me.

Krueger was brought to me because the trucker was turned into the police for animal cruelty. The police told him the dog either goes to The Pet Hotel, or they would seize the dog. Nobody, including the cops, informed me of this.

She said the last time her ex was in town, she saw him punch the dog in the head. The gouge on Krueger's forehead was from the ring the trucker wore. Every abuse that happened to the dog, the woman said, was her ex's doing.

Why did I believe her? Because Krueger told me to believe her.

The woman asked if she could see the dog, and Krueger went right to her for petting. As we continued to chat, he wandered the yard. Then the woman set her less than three-year-old daughter down on the ground. The dog saw the girl and headed to her as if shot from a cannon.

I started to intercept him, but the woman turned to me, shrugged, and said, "He's not going to do anything to her." As Krueger put the brakes on hard, the tot reached out and held onto his back. Together they slowly walked the yard.

The woman explained, "That's why he treats the dog so badly. He wanted a mean Rottweiler, and this dog isn't one."

When the trucker came back, it was without money. I told him he couldn't take the dog without paying. Then I made him an offer. "The dog spends so much time here, why don't I just buy him from you?"

I gave the trucker a couple of hundred bucks on top of credit for the boarding bill, and now Kruger was mine. When his ex-wife called again, she said, "Beware. He will steal that dog back." Sure enough, a couple of months later, the man showed up asking about the dog.

I told him I had Krueger neutered before placing him with relatives in another state. I could tell he wasn't happy that I had his dog fixed. I never heard from or saw him again.

Krueger was a good dog, and I could have kept him, but it was in the dog's best interest to be out of reach of this man.

After I rescued Krueger and before I sent him out of state, I renamed him Sentry. Yes, he was the same dog who frightened the meter reader.

If you run a boarding facility, you may occasionally find yourself in a situation like this with a dog who needs rescue. At the same time, you don't want to become an unpaid humane society.

As you generate business and your kennel is full much of the time, you can start raising your prices. It's basic supply and demand. When there is too much demand, the price goes up. If you do this, you will also make more money and turn fewer people away.

As you start making and saving more, start thinking about what to do next. My plan, had I stayed, was to expand The Pet Hotel to include The Pet Store, The Pet Groomer, The Pet Trainer, and The Pet Vet, all on this five-acre property.

There were five vets in town, and the bulk of their business was cattle and horses. One vet, however, was interested in doing more with small animals. We discussed the possibility of linking his practice with The Pet Hotel. No money would be exchanged, but he would be at the kennel one day a week, and available for occasional meet-and-greets throughout the year.

You might be able to make a similar arrangement with a vet where you are, especially with a vet new to your area. It can help the vet boost business and spread your reputation as *the* place to board dogs and cats.

In The Pet Store, I wanted to carry dog food, supplies, and dog treats. One brand of dog food I wanted to carry was especially promising. The food was medium in price, yet it compared favorably with the most expensive brands in ingredients and no one in the area carried it.

With The Pet Groomer, I planned to work my way up, starting with one grooming station and hiring a groomer to come in one or two days a week. For The Pet Trainer, I would combine training with Young Dog Play Days to teach basic commands.

If you have an extended family, you can do something similar. Say your sister wants to learn to groom and her daughter is thinking about becoming a vet. You might bring them into the business. Perhaps your daughter or son wants to train dogs. You get the idea. There are many possibilities for expansion.

Had I stayed, I might have put a kennel with runs somewhere in back. I also would have increased the size and spaciousness of the cattery.

It's all a matter of progression and cost. Do you have the business to support a new expense? Then expand. In this business, your problems may not be solved by throwing money at them. It isn't like *Field of Dreams*—build it, and they will come. But once you see demand, you can develop a way to take advantage of it.

Your rules, procedures, and ways of running your business will lead to success. You might start out one way, then change course a bit. The rules of the 9 to 5 world won't always work. People with somewhere to go head out early and get back late. Coming home at 7 p.m., they want to unload their vehicle and pick up their dog half an hour later.

Your goal should be to give each dog the care and attention it needs to be safe and content, while remembering it's not the only dog you have to care for.

To build a pet hotel from scratch, it wouldn't make sense to begin with a large state-of-the-art facility unless demand is guaranteed. If you have a little ingenuity and stick-to-itiveness, you can figure things out starting with what you have. If you have previous experience as a volunteer at a humane society or dog shelter, or as a vet's assistant, it will put you miles ahead of me when I started.

You need more than business knowledge to run a boarding facility. You need dog knowledge, and there is no way to get all the information you need except through experience as things occur.

It's rained four days straight, and you have 18 dogs in the kennel: wet dogs, wet dog crap, and dogs that don't want to go potty in the rain. There might be dogs who can't be exercised because it is raining, and they are getting destructive.

If you start small and grow gradually, you will figure all this out.

If you still think you want to build a kennel, my final suggestion is this: draw up plans, including measurements, on paper. At this stage, the plans need to be good, not perfect.

The first decision is how many pens (or pens with runs) you will have. You can start as small as boarding one dog in your own home on weekends. The maximum number of pens for a solo owner is about 20. I started with 13 pens for dogs and 9 for cats. Eventually, I expanded the kennel to handle a maximum of 27 dogs and 14 cats, but that was only over holidays, and it involved using temporary and portable pens.

Plan your workday. Plan where the food and water will come from, how you will do outs, how you will exercise the dogs, where you will meet pet owners, where you will store supplies. Price it out. Add 10% to your estimate just in case.

Figure out how many boardings that represents at your tentative price point. Before you hammer the first nail, make the best estimate you can. This is your dry run. Many books on this topic are written as "how-to," but there is more to this than how to. Do you still want that kennel? Then immerse yourself in the subject.

I decided to do it. It wasn't that big an investment. It was just putting things together with a little sweat equity. My daily routine may sound busy, yet throughout the day I had time to do the things I wanted to do.

Plan for the ordinary day. That smooth, happy, ordinary day. Owners drop dogs off, you feed them, you take them out, they get playtime. The owner comes back and picks up a contented dog.

That's what you want. The ordinary day.

Some of the things that went wrong for me might have been avoided. The warnings I give, the cautionary tales I've told, have only one purpose: to enable you to have one ordinary day after another.

A few years after I left, someone who knew about my business went whole hog and overspent on building, construction, and staff. They could have succeeded boarding dogs, but they went way too big. Their estimate of the market and what they could charge was way off. Instead of having a small failure, they had a huge failure.

The mistake they made was almost literally a million-dollar mistake. They didn't know what they were doing and they overbuilt. They needed a facility which matched their market, but they built for a premium market without enough people willing to pay the premium price.

You can't make a mistake by going small. Simple, small, and efficient to begin with. You can always expand. When it works, you can expand smartly. If you don't know the body of water, don't jump in headfirst.

The risk to you, emotionally and personally and financially, is less if you start small.

Finally, let me share a conviction with you. There is something noble about caring for dogs. What you are thinking about doing has great emotional value to people and to their companion animals. Because I love animals, I want there to be good places where people can board their dogs.

Over 150 years ago George Vest, a lawyer and senator from Missouri, represented a man whose dog was killed by another man.

In his closing arguments, Vest said, "The one absolutely unselfish friend that man can have in this selfish world, the one that never deserts him, the one that never proves ungrateful or treacherous, is his dog...when riches take wings, and reputation falls to pieces, he is as constant in his love as the sun in its journey through the heavens."

This ends my story. Your story begins in the next part of the book. It is about understanding your local dog community, starting and marketing your services, and managing your business.

I hope you find boarding dogs as rewarding as I have.

PART FOUR

STARTING YOUR BUSINESS

Throughout this book, I've assumed you don't have half a million dollars or more to spend on opening your business. If you did, you might be talking to a boarding franchiser. And if you bought a franchise, they would tell you exactly what to do, even when to turn the lights on in the morning.

If you start your own independent kennel, you will have to figure out those things for yourself.

But before you plunge ahead, there is another issue to consider. Are you sure where you fit in the dog world?

There are so many options: dog walking, in-home pet sitting, doggie day care, training, overnight dog boarding, and grooming.

I suggest exploring the professional associations in the field. It will broaden your knowledge, and as you will see, professional associations can give you access to things like group rate insurance, accounting resources, marketing materials, and more.

From the groups below, you will get more ideas, and the ones most relevant to you will offer new avenues to explore. The list is not all-inclusive, but it's a good starting point.

Professional Associations
National Association of Professional Pet Sitters
https://petsitters.org/

The International Boarding & Pet Services Association (IBPSA)
https://www.ibpsa.com/

Pet Sitters International
https://www.petsit.com/

The Association of Professional Dog Trainers
https://apdt.com/

Certification Council for Professional Dog Trainers
https://www.ccpdt.org/

National Dog Groomers Association of America
https://nationaldoggroomers.com/

Canadian Professional Pet Stylists
https://canpropetstylists.ca

Another source of help is the various kennel clubs. They offer a wealth of training tips, courses, and advice. Much of it is free.

Kennel Clubs
American Kennel Club
https://www.akc.org/

Canadian Kennel Club
https://www.ckc.ca/en

The (UK) Kennel Club
https://www.thekennelclub.org.uk/

As you know from reading up to this point, I believe in three general principles:

- Start small
- Play the long game
- Keep thinking in terms of the next step

If I added something more, it would be this. Expect some wasted effort and expense. Don't fret about it. It's simply part of learning anything new. At the same time, don't buy expensive courses or training until you really understand the field, and maybe not even then.

In the beginning days of your business, you may feel clumsy and awkward. But every day you will get faster and more comfortable with what you do.

The first time you handle a nervous dog, the first time you give medicine to a new dog, the first time you handle more than one dog on a leash at the same time, you may be uneasy. But before long, it will be familiar. Confidence will come with experience.

There are three key areas where you need to develop yourself:

- knowledge of your local dog community
- marketing your business
- managing your business

Your customers pay for the care, safety, and pleasant experience you give their dog, but if you are new to the field, it may pay to get more experience first. Get your feet wet. Get involved in the dog community.

Your Local Dog Community

You love dogs. That's a given. You understand dogs and their behavior, and you are always anxious to learn more.

But you also need to connect with the dog community where you live, for several reasons. You need to know who is out there in your space so you learn from them, so they can learn about you, and so you know who to recommend for the services you do not provide.

Chances are you won't know all the available resources until you research your local dog community. There are people and organizations who can help you. You may even find a mentor, and you will meet local people with connections to national organizations.

There are people who show dogs, train dogs, and go to dog shows, and there may be local online dog forums. Any of these resources may help you.

Let me give you a concrete example.

I currently live in a city with a population under 200,000. Like every city, it has a dog community.

There is a community college that offers short dog courses (24 hours of instruction spread over six weeks). The courses are modestly priced, each costing barely more than a day's pay at a low-level job. They are taught by an experienced veterinarian who is a companion animal specialist.

One course is about starting a pet-sitting business. Another is about basic veterinary assistant skills. A third course teaches more advanced skills for veterinary assistants, and a fourth course is about canine reproduction.

These courses are also offered online.

Completion of courses like these can give you a leg up in attracting clients. You will learn about everything from flea control to pet emergencies, from canine blood work to nutrition, from vaccinations to handling owners. Along the way you will learn more about injuries, parasites like roundworms and heartworms, and helping owners say goodbye to a treasured dog.

My city has an all-volunteer club which offers classes in puppy socialization, home and public manners, obedience, tricks, agility, rally, scent work, and tracking.

There is an animal advocacy organization, open one day a week, that offers low cost spaying and neutering for dogs and cats. There is a humane society, and there is a rescue group that runs an independent no-kill shelter. All these organizations welcome volunteers.

Volunteering will increase your knowledge base and put you in touch with local people in the field. It can help you establish yourself in the field. At the same time, you don't want to get sidetracked from your main goal, which is to start a successful dog boarding business.

As you investigate the resources in your community, you will also learn more about dog walking, in-home pet sitting, boarding kennels, puppy socialization, dog training, and grooming.

It will give you knowledge of the best vets in your city, and enable you to make solid recommendations to clients.

Researching your local dog community is a powerful way to boost your business. Find the people who can help you. If boarding and pet care are right for you, this will feel exciting.

Before you start boarding dogs, however, you must decide exactly what services you will offer. That's the first question to answer.

The second question is, how will I market my business?

Marketing

Unfortunately, dogs can't buy your services. Only people can. So like it or not, you have to learn about marketing.

There is an old saying in the field that only 50% of marketing works, but no one knows which 50%. That's the basic problem with marketing. But I think you can simplify marketing by looking at it this way.

Marketing is about being top of mind in the minds of potential customers.

Marketing is also about consistency over time and persistence over time, but it is primarily about being top of mind with potential customers.

I am probably going to give you too much information, so remember, I'm a big advocate of starting small and building over the long term. Start with what is easiest for you.

We can divide marketing into two parts: content marketing and advertising, both paid and unpaid. We will talk about advertising first.

Unpaid advertising is being active in the dog community. It is being active in organizations and connecting with influencers. It is being listed as a business by Google and Bing. It is starting a Facebook business page.

Paid advertising is buying space in a venue. The space may be physical, as in a shoppers newspaper, or virtual, as in a paid web listing. If you have your own business website, that is really paid advertising because it costs money, even though it belongs to you.

But before you start advertising in any way, think about your brand.

What is a brand? A brand is how you portray yourself to the public.

It is how you want people to feel about you. What they think about you won't make them call. What they feel about you will. The more you can tie yourself to positive emotions, the more your business will thrive.

For your dog boarding business, you want to establish yourself as knowledgeable, warm, caring, and professional.

Among other things, establishing a brand means using the same typeface, the same logo, and the same colors in all your materials, printed or online. Your brand extends to the feel of your Facebook page and to the feel of your website (though you may not have one at this point).

Onboarding a new client is the time when long-term relationships are cemented. Giving owners something tangible and useful will connect them to you and help keep you top of mind.

That is why I suggest creating a welcome packet. A welcome packet includes information about you and all your services. If you have a newsletter, a copy goes there as well. Put everything in a good-looking folder. The welcome folder is also the place for pet parents to put their copy of your boarding agreement.

The other part of marketing is content marketing, and it is one of the most effective ways to be top of mind with potential clients.

But what is it?

Content marketing means creating free stuff.

In content marketing, you create engaging and helpful information and put it out to the people you want to draw to your service.

Content marketing assumes that, while you will reach many people, only a minority will become your customers. That's okay, because when you reach enough people, your business can become a success.

The content you create may be in any form. It can be Facebook posts, information on your website, or information in a newsletter or flyer. It can be an occasional blog post, especially one aimed at your specific target market. It can be in a column in a daily or weekly newspaper, or in a shopper newspaper.

The content you create might be about the best places to walk dogs. It might list three ways to encourage positive behavior in a dog. It might be seven keys to understanding your dog's behavior. It can be about new canine products. It can be about anything.

In general, content marketing is not about you and your services. It is about giving value to potential clients. But in all content marketing, you will include your full contact information—business name, address, phone, email, and services offered.

It's not build it, and they will come. It's help them, and enough of them will come to build your business. So offer something useful, entertaining, or inspirational. This is a soft sell. It is giving people a gift. It is letting people understand why you are the go-to place.

When many of us sit down to write content, we draw a blank. That's why I recommend *Master Content Marketing* and *Master Content Strategy* by Pamela Wilson. These books can give you many ideas for your Facebook page, website, newsletter, blog, or brochure.

And if you are unsure of your writing skills, hire a proofreader on Fiverr to edit your copy.

I always recommend using Facebook, because it is free and because, as I have mentioned, it is a huge search engine. On Facebook, you can explain what your business is, who it serves, and offer articles helpful to dog owners. Some people on Facebook will type in "dog boarding" and their city. Make sure your business comes up in search results.

You can use other social media that appeals to you, but remember that social media can be a huge time waster that does not build your business.

Brainstorming ideas can lead to imaginative approaches to marketing.

Let me give you a demonstration, using my own experience.

I had friends, a couple, whose friend was running for a seat on the city council. It was a nonpartisan election, and their friend had less name recognition than other candidates for office.

The election was on a Tuesday. The Sunday before the election, this couple walked a precinct that was mostly apartment buildings, near where they lived.

To help their friend, they went door to door with a nice flyer which included the candidate's picture.

They attached the flyer to the doorknobs on over a thousand apartments, and it took most of Sunday afternoon. They didn't talk to the people they ran into. They were too shy for that. They simply smiled, said hello, and continued distributing their flyers.

Amazingly, their friend won that precinct. To me, the best explanation is that, when most people went to the polls, one candidate was top of mind.

Let me give you another example. A different friend was an assistant manager at a restaurant. On his day off he was expected to distribute business cards, which were also discount cards, door-to-door. He hated it, and he merely placed the cards between the front door and the door jamb of each house.

Because the discount cards acted like cash, each was attached to the check as proof the discount was redeemed. When the manager checked the register each night, he was stunned by how many customers used the cards to reduce their bill.

How would I apply these two examples to my dog boarding business, if I started one today?

I would design a flyer with useful information (which is content marketing) for dog owners. The information might be the 10 best things to do if your dog is lost. When a dog is lost, many people simply jump in their car and start looking.

They often forget other highly useful things, like asking their postal carrier to watch for the dog, contacting area vets with the pet's description and picture, repeatedly calling animal shelters, and posting a reward to online neighborhood groups.

The flyer would contain all my business information and services, but it would not contain any direct solicitations for business.

You may think you are above going door to door. I understand that. I'm an introvert and the idea makes me a little uneasy, but if the neighborhood is safe, why not? And, if you are ashamed of your car, park it around the block.

Before distributing my flyer, I would identify several reasonably affluent neighborhoods where the houses were close together. On Monday, I would devote one hour to delivering the flyer to 60 houses. On Tuesday, I would deliver the flyer to another 60 houses. I would do the same on Wednesday and Thursday.

One hour per day, four days in one week, not counting travel time. The total hours of actual work would be four hours. I would skip a month and then repeat the process to the same group of homes. This time my flyer might be about maximizing the health of your dog.

Then I would skip a month and return with a flyer on why I love caring for dogs or listing my favorite dog books. Each time I would be dressed in clean, professional looking clothes. Neat, but not fancy.

I would not offer discounts in the flyer. Although you might in special circumstances offer a discount, your business should not be built on discounts. It should be built on trust in your competence.

Would my idea work? I frankly don't know. I would not know until I tried it, but I could easily tell if it did.

I have the addresses of the 240 homes I canvased. If a dog boarded from any one of those addresses, it would be fair to assume the strategy worked.

Distributing the flyers took 12 hours total. The flyers, done in Microsoft Word or for free at Canva.com, would not cost much. I could tally the number of new boarders from those addresses and calculate my return on investment, or ROI.

I could also assume that many people who boarded would become repeat customers, and others would board later, when they had the need. So my calculation of ROI would probably be low.

As you recall, I recommend always asking customers how they heard about you. In this case, the customer's addresses would be all the proof I needed.

In a separate campaign in another neighborhood, I might include a refrigerator magnet with my newsletter. Refrigerator magnets are cheap, and people have an innate bias against throwing away something they might use.

You get the idea. Keep brainstorming ways to improve your business, especially ways which do not have a huge cash outlay. If something doesn't work, drop it and develop another strategy.

Once you understand what works for you, marketing will become automatic. And as you become better known, it will become less necessary.

Another aspect of marketing is focus. Ask yourself, what is my niche? Who am I targeting?

Are you aiming to provide daycare for owners at work...overnight boarding for people on vacation...or do you want to encourage long-term boarders, from pet parents who travel a lot.

Vary your ad copy, flyers, and website based on who you want to attract. When one thing doesn't work, try another.

A final point about marketing is this. I have used the words "customer" and "client" interchangeably, but I suggest you look at everyone who comes to you as a client, not a customer.

What's the difference? A customer buys a service. A client is someone whose best interests you have at heart. Make the pet parents who come to you your clients, and they will become your ambassadors.

Starting and Managing Your Business

A friend of mine does the taxes for her sister in Florida. This sister has an in-home dog sitting business with far-flung clients. What my friend immediately noticed is that her sister is hardly making any money. Travel and needless expenses eat up most of her income.

You don't want to be like that. You want a business that is efficient, with an accounting system that is easy to maintain and gives you an accurate picture of how you are doing.

Let me say another word about accounting systems. There is nothing wrong with starting with a paper-based system. Online bookstores sell income and expense ledgers for dog businesses. They also sell schedulers for boarding, sitting, and dog walking.

Until you are making serious money, avoid pet accounting software that comes with a monthly charge. If you are familiar with Excel, you can set up a custom spreadsheet to handle your income, expenses, and scheduling. Or you can do the same with Google Sheets, which is free, and has many simple tutorials.

Now is also a good time to think about personal habits you have, like procrastination, that will get in the way of success. If this is an issue for you, an excellent book on changing habits is James Clear's *Atomic Habits*.

For me, learning about dogs was a pleasure; learning about business was more of a chore. But it was a necessary chore.

Some days you may not "feel like it." That's why you need a plan and a structure to keep your life and your business running on the rails. When your self-discipline is flagging, good organization and a routine will keep you moving in the right direction.

Having a workable, effective system in the beginning will save time and keep your business on track.

The question is, how should I begin?

First, check the exact zoning restrictions for your business address. That is done with your local unit of government.

Then, if you are in any state in the United States, there is a Small Business Development Center ready to help. Google "Small Business Development Center" plus the name of your state.

These business centers are the place for the most up-to-date information for starting a business in your city, county, and state. Typically, they are affiliated with a state university, and they offer courses and workshops.

They either have complete information on licenses, fees, business registration, and taxes, or they have links to other levels of government which do. The services of small business development centers, including consulting, are free or low cost.

The equivalent service in Canada is found at Canada.ca, the Canadian Government's official site. In the UK, the official site is Gov.uk.

Business development centers will give you a handle on the legal side of the business. But how can you begin boarding?

Since 2011, there have been pet sitting and boarding services which are the equivalent of Uber and Lyft. At first, it was Rover and DogVacay. Then Rover acquired DogVacay. Today, the best-known companies are Rover.com and Wag!.

If you work with these companies, you will be an independent contractor. The advantage to them is that making you an independent contractor frees them from all kinds of legal obligations. The advantage to you is, as an independent contractor, you can get clients from them while simultaneously starting your own independent kennel business.

Both Rover and Wag! offer resources that can help you learn the basics of the business. Rover, for example, offers Rover 101, which is training for newcomers on how to create a polished business profile, how to set rates, how to book stays, and how to appeal to customers.

Don't look at these companies as your competition. Think of the ways they can boost your business.

Rover and Wag! can help you get started, but an independent kennel can make substantially more money than someone working solely for Rover or Wag!. In addition, an established kennel can offer more consistent care than people in the gig economy, who may be here today and gone tomorrow.

You might also check out Veronica Boutelle's books on the business side of pet care.

It is not possible to give one-size-fits-all advice. Some of you may have a day job and want to start with Rover, boarding on weekends. Some of you may start building a homemade kennel on your own property. Some of you may be thinking of renting or buying a commercial property.

The main point is to find a spot that appeals to you, do the research, and begin. I am not saying you have to expand. You might be quite comfortable at a beginning level or intermediate level. But there are people who have begun as a small boarding kennel and expanded to include virtually every service that can be offered to pet owners.

You don't absolutely need a website yet, but if you have a unique name for your business, and that domain name is available, buy it before someone else does. The domain name should match your business' name. For example, if your business is Fairview Dog Care, you want to buy FairviewDogCare.com.

You can check domain name availability and purchase domain names through sites like GoDaddy.com. While it is possible to have a free website, if you own your own site, it will give you more control and look more professional.

Once you own a domain name and decide you want a website, you will need a host for the site. Hosts, like SiteGround.com, are simply servers where your site resides. You can have a web designer design your site or you can download a template and do it yourself.

It looks more professional to have an email address with your domain name. Joan@FairviewDogCare.com. This can be arranged through your website host, usually for free, or from Google or Microsoft for a monthly fee.

A dog boarding website does not need to be big. It needs to be professional.

Your website exists for one reason. To drive customers to your business. It needs to carry out the theme of your brand. If you write articles and post them on your website, you will be providing keywords that help people find the site.

If you regularly write helpful articles on pet care and behavior, you will be giving visitors a reason to return, even if they don't need your services today.

Use images. Include frequently asked questions. List dog friendly places in your town. Make recommendations on collars, toys, or products you like.

Don't forget to include social proof, which is a fancy name for testimonials from satisfied customers. Most people don't want to be the first to act. If they know others use your services, they will feel more comfortable calling you.

A professional boarding website has:

- Simple navigation
- Directions
- Bullet points
- Short paragraphs
- Pictures of happy dogs
- Social proof – testimonials
- Contact information on every page

It may also have:

- Helpful articles
- Book recommendations
- Answers to common questions

Your website should link to your Facebook page and your Facebook page should link to your website.

Here are more ideas.

When a boarder arrives, always greet the dog first.

In my vet's reception area, there is a sign reading, "Today welcoming..." then it lists each dog that is expected. The dog names are in colored chalk, and pet owners love it when you welcome their dog.

Thank your customers. Perhaps even send them a thank-you note after the first boarding. It will set you apart. Tell your clients why you enjoyed their dog, and mention one or two things the dog did while in your care. Always, always, always repeat the dog's name.

People won't care if you sometimes forget their name. They expect to be known as Brandi's mom or Rex's dad. But they want to feel their dog is important to you.

If you do an email newsletter periodically, make it short and lively. Make it worth reading. You can send professional-looking email from services like MailerLite. MailerLite.com is free for the first 1,000 people who subscribe to your newsletter.

There are aspects to dog businesses that are generally true.

If you offer dog walking, often that business trails off during the holidays and vacation times. Those times, however, are peak times for dog boarding.

Overnight boarding tends to be sporadic, while walking and daycare services tend to be regular and predictable.

Because some people get divorced, change jobs, or travel for long periods of time, long-term boarding can stabilize your business and even out the ups and downs. Though you may need to offer lower rates for long-term boarders, these pets are usually easy to handle because they "know the drill" at your facility.

If you successfully train dogs, you can run through clients quickly. That will create a constant need to replenish your supply of clients. But if you board and train, training is an added service which can boost the bill.

When you begin, set your fees at least at the average for your area. If you have more certifications or experience, charge a little more. Good dog owners don't want the cheapest, they want the best. Undercharge now, and it will be harder to raise rates later.

When you increase your rates, let clients know in advance and don't apologize. People understand that the cost of everything goes up.

When you outline your policies, state them confidently. Act as if each is simply the standard practice in your field.

Make quality standards a part of your daily routine.

There will be pain points in developing your business. The first might be transitioning from your day job. The next might be when you are faced with the need or desire to expand. A third might be when you realize you need to hire staff.

That's just life. There will always be new challenges and problems to solve. Yet there are deep satisfactions to working with dogs. The writer Edward Hoagland once said that the point of owning dogs is not to train them to be like us. It is to train us to be more like them.

Dogs put us in touch with the part of ourselves we lost in childhood.

Epilogue

If you enjoyed the book and learned something, please consider leaving a review where you bought the book. It would mean so much to me.

Sarah

About the Author

Sarah Clark boarded more than 45 different dog breeds in her pet boarding business, in addition to countless mixed breed dogs.

She has been a pet parent to a black Lab, three Golden Retrievers, two Cairn Terriers, two Rottweilers, a Samoyed, and a Shih Tzu. And three cats.

Most of her pets were rescues.

Made in the USA
Monee, IL
02 April 2022

93989668R00066